THE LEADERSHIP LIBRARY

V O L U M E   4

WHEN IT'S TIME TO MOVE

Other books in The Leadership Library

Well-Intentioned Dragons by Marshall Shelley

Liberating the Leader's Prayer Life by Terry Muck

Clergy Couples in Crisis by Dean Merrill

THE LEADERSHIP LIBRARY

Volume

4

When It's Time to Move

A Guide to Changing Churches

Paul D. Robbins

Carol Stream, Illinois

WORD BOOKS
PUBLISHER
WACO, TEXAS

A DIVISION OF
WORD, INCORPORATED

WHEN IT'S TIME TO MOVE

Preface, chapter introductions, and ancillary copy © 1985 Christianity Today, Inc.
Chapter 1 © 1985 Calvin C. Ratz
Chapter 2 © 1983 Ben Patterson
Chapter 3 © 1984 Douglas G. Scott
Chapter 4 © 1983 Douglas J. Rumford
Chapter 5 © 1980 Norman Shawchuck
Chapter 6 © 1980 Roy C. Price
Chapter 7 © 1980 Em A. Griffin
Chapter 8 © 1981 C. Neil Strait
Chapter 9 © 1985 Carl F. George
Chapter 10 © 1981 Eugene H. Peterson
Chapter 11 © 1983 James D. Berkley

A LEADERSHIP/Word Book. Copublished by Christianity Today, Inc. and Word, Inc.
Distributed by Word Books

Cover art by Joe Van Severen

Library of Congress Cataloging-in-Publication Data

When it's time to move.

  (The Leadership Library; v. 4)
  1. Clergy—Relocation—Addresses, essays, lectures.
I. Robbins, Paul D., 1936- . II. Series.
BV664.W47 1985   253'.2   85-21310
ISBN 0-917463-07-2

Printed in the United States of America

CONTENTS

71958

PREFACE

Four years ago Jim Railson (not his actual name) came to his present church with his wife and baby son. Full of enthusiasm and love for God, they were determined to make this first senior pastorate a success. Then Jim began to discover things:

• The previous pastor had not left for another call, as he had said. He had left because the elders discovered his adulterous relationship with a divorcée in the church.

• A mortgage payment of $11,000 was due in thirty days, or the church would lose its building.

• The church was deeply in debt. The previous pastor had led the congregation of 125 into a $500,000 mortgage on an old, single-story building in an undesirable part of town. Monthly payments: $5,000.

• The church had never been officially organized, so it was not tax-exempt.

• A balloon payment of $235,000 was due in two years, which no one on the board had known anything about.

• Real estate firms in the community wouldn't handle their property because they considered it unsalable.

"The problems were monumental, all the more so because I

had no inkling they existed. When we candidated, we stayed with the church chairman at his beautiful suburban home, complete with swimming pool. He never said a thing about financial problems. Everything looked solid to me."

And to many in the church, too. But as people realized the situation, they began to leave, further depleting already inadequate resources. "I found myself facing more discouragement and depression than I ever thought possible," remembers Jim. "Most of my prayer time was spent crying in self-pity. My positive praise dwindled away.

"I realized the problems were not my fault. But why would God lead me to this place? Why didn't I have the sense to see them beforehand? What skills did I have to solve them now that I was here?

"I struggled against people, city government, financial burdens, inadequate workers, guilt over lack of personal family time, and petty sins that began to creep into my own life. I was swimming against an overpowering tide. The Bible held many promises of power, but none of them seemed to apply to me. I felt totally alone."

Because of his sense of loyalty and stubborn persistence, Jim eventually managed to work the church out of the pit where he found it. Today, the church has a decent chance of survival.

But what of the four long years? What were the lessons he learned?

"I could have come to this church much better prepared than I did. I could have asked better questions about the situation. I could have been more aware of the resources in the congregation—people who could have helped me if I had known how to approach them. I could have been more aware of my own weaknesses and thus avoided some of their consequences.

"But I lived through it, and I know other pastors have lived through similar experiences. Perhaps others can learn through our stories."

Perhaps they can. The average tenure of a local-church

leader in the United States is under five years. For young pastors, frequent changes can be especially difficult. Inexperience makes every unexpected revelation even more of a challenge.

But the problem is not solely faced by seminarians. Many a veteran of twenty years has found himself hip-deep in the flood of surprises that threaten to wash over any new pastor. How he handles it depends on preparation, both vocational and spiritual.

Perhaps more than most professionals, the minister is vulnerable to tangled situations. The ministry is a unique combination of spiritual and secular calling. On one level (the most important), obedience and commitment are primary. The material realities common to other professions must take a back seat. Salary level and climbing the corporate ladder are not the starting points.

But the "secular" questions must be answered sometime. Many a spiritual question has been pushed to the background because a fundamental financial or vocational question hasn't been adequately dealt with.

Theologians have long recognized this dual nature of the call to ministry. John Calvin described the two elements in his *Institutes*. The first is an internal acknowledgment that God demands we go into full-time ministry: "the secret call of which every minister is conscious in himself before God." The second is the call of a denomination or church to a specific locale or venue: "the external call that belongs to the public order of the church."

Both the secret and external calls need to be present in order for a pastorate to work. God chose Barnabas and Paul and Titus. But the local church validated those calls by providing venues for their ministries and thousands more after them. The call came from God, but the church blessed the choice.

God's voice creates several of the life-rearranging questions facing the church-changing pastor. The local church's anointing (or lack thereof) gives rise to the others. All serve to create turning points in the pastor's life that would be crucial enough if only a career were at stake. Add the spiritual dimension of call, and they become not only life-changing but psyche-splitting. God's power descends on a pastor in a special way, making the ministry a vocation like no other.

The change points of ministry affect everyone who serves. Not everyone is affected by them all, or perhaps to the same extreme as Jim Railson faced them in his new church. So we can't just tell one incident and hope to be fair to the complexity of the issue. To begin to adequately cover the topic, we need to hear the voices of many, the experiences of young and old. Each has part of the story to tell.

Over the years, writers for LEADERSHIP Journal have talked about the difficult questions surrounding a change of church:

• How do I know when it's time to resign? Perhaps this is the most wrenching question of all. Can there possibly be any formula to tell when a ministry is over?

• How do I go about the process of candidating for a church? Church polity makes a big difference here, of course. But some aspects are pandenominational.

• What are the immediate issues that will face me in a new church? Three seem to be crucial: building trust, establishing authority, and deciding on a personal ministry style.

• Does the pastor changing churches face special psychological pitfalls?

• And finally, what resources do I have to cope with these problems? In chapter 10, Eugene Peterson talks about the spiritual lifestyle of the pastorate.

In the following pages we present the thoughts of ministers who have changed churches. What emerges is a picture of the ministry. Not an easy or glamorous story, but one filled with the excitement of serving God and a true sense of importance and challenge. These are people dedicated to doing God's will in perhaps the toughest place possible—the local church. It's an important picture, because the local church is God's voice and witness in a world that seldom listens or sees.

—*Paul Robbins*
Christianity Today, Inc.

ONE

THE LONELIEST CHOICE OF ALL

When I have learned to do the Father's will, I shall have fully realized my vocation on earth.

CARLO CARRETTO

The relocation saga begins for most pastors with a bedeviling question: "Is it time to resign my present church?" The future of one's ministry, the trust of a congregation, the needs of spouse and children, and the opinion of peers all seem to heighten the emotional stakes and blur objectivity.

In this first chapter, Calvin C. Ratz writes candidly about the decision that brought him to his present pastorate at Abbotsford Pentecostal Assembly in British Columbia, an hour outside of Vancouver. Now in his forties, married, and the father of two children, Ratz has faced the shall-we-move? dilemma enough times in his ministerial career to have sorted out the factors and identified important questions to consider.

I t happened while we were unloading the car and trailer. Our family had just spent a week sailing on Lake Champlain in Vermont, and we were in the middle of trucking dirty clothes, ice coolers, and camping gear back into our home in Montreal when the phone rang.

A man three thousand miles away whom I had never met, the chairman of a pulpit search committee, came to the point quickly: Would I consider meeting with his group to discuss becoming senior pastor of their church?

If that board could have seen me at that moment, they would have questioned their decision. I hadn't shaved in a week; I was sweaty, dirty, and wearing a ragged pair of shorts and no shirt. I was in no condition to deal with a major spiritual decision.

Once again it was time to go through the agonizing process of determining whether to leave a congregation and assume new responsibilities elsewhere. I hadn't sought the invitation; it had come to me. It would be a personal choice: only I could make it. Yet my wife and two children were deeply involved. Two congregations would be affected, and more. What about my commitment to co-chair the upcoming Leighton Ford Crusade in Montreal? Like it or not, I was again being thrown into a reassessment of God's plan for my ministry.

How is such a decision made? What process does a pastor follow in coming to grips with perhaps the most crucial choice of pastoral life? And how do you do it quickly?

When an invitation comes out of the blue with a sudden phone call, the board usually wants to know within forty-eight hours if you're willing to talk further. You may be able to do some fast scouting during those hours, calling colleagues who know the new church situation. But more than that, you have to pray and think fast. To say, "Yes, I'll discuss it with you" means, for me, that I am at least *prepared* to leave my present church. I don't want to lead them on.

And the deciding is lonely. I admire pastors whose openness permits them to share major personal decisions with their people. But I can't do that at resignation time. Breaking away from a church is delicate for everyone concerned. Most people don't like to see an indecisive or unsettled pastor. Congregations need to be protected if there is going to be a pastoral change. They need to know their pastor is leaving because he has received divine guidance that God is directing him elsewhere.

During that unexpected phone call from Abbotsford, I asked the usual questions. It took about twenty minutes to find out the size of the congregation, church finances, indebtedness, size of present staff, facilities, and previous pastors. I'd been through the process before and knew the information I needed.

Later, while alone in prayer, I faced the other side of the coin: leaving Montreal. Was my work done? Did God want me to accomplish more (or learn more) here? What about my unfulfilled dreams and plans for this church? I had no desire to leave. There were no major problems. I loved both the city and the congregation. The people were kind and responsive.

In the previous eighteen months, I had received inquiries from other churches. Each had been larger, offering better conditions and in some ways better prospects for building a large congregation. I had treated each one seriously and prayerfully. However, I had declined each of them.

But what about this one? Was it time to break away for a new challenge? The fact that I could look back and feel good about the previous change points of my life meant nothing now. Would this be the misstep I would live to regret? The next month was difficult, but the choice was finally made. Within two months we left for British Columbia.

A Direct Line to Heaven?

If you ask people why they move from one pastorate to another, you get a string of clichés and a pot full of piety. "I just knew God wanted me to leave." Or, "We prayed and had a gut feeling it was God's will." As with most clichés, there is an aspect of truth here. We do want that inner conviction, that witness of the Spirit that we are doing the right thing.

But I've been around long enough to know that God, like the Devil, gets blamed for a lot of decisions he had little to do with. The truth is, we pastors do not always have a direct line to heaven. Nor are we always listening carefully to what the Spirit is saying. A great many human factors figure in the decision to leave one church for another.

It's easy to think it's God's will to move on when the invitation is to a larger church, the salary and benefits are better, and you're having problems where you are. But greener pastures are not necessarily God's will. He may simply be using that invitation to test our resolve and determination to carry on.

How Long Is Long Enough?

We are all aware that some pastors accomplish a great deal by staying in one church a long time. My father-in-law's most productive years came near the end of a twenty-four-year pastorate. In many church circles, pastors seem to be staying longer than in previous times. This appears to be a healthy development. It's significant that most larger churches have been established and built by those who have stayed for decades.

Knowing this made me want to stay longer in Montreal. Shouldn't I be the leader who would take this church on to greatness?

But on the other hand, some pastors stay too long. They hang on when in fact their ministry has peaked or been completed. Some are incapable of leading the church to its next plateau. They may have the ability to pastor a church of 150 effectively and build it to 300, but they are incapable of administering and leading a church beyond that. Yet they stay. They fail to recognize their own limitations. Their ego says they can do it all.

A great deal of insecurity is wrapped up in overstaying: the anxiety in facing a new city and congregation . . . the fear of breaking relationships and starting over.

There is no simple formula for how long to stay before moving on. Who of us can declare unequivocally, "So-and-so stayed too long" or "left too soon"? We may have our private opinions, but we also know we could be mistaken.

If we are less than sure about the other fellow's tenure, how much more about our own? Each pastorate is different. Pioneering a congregation is not the same as caring for an established church. Rural, suburban, and inner-city churches differ. Our ministerial gifts vary. The person with a teaching/pastoral ministry will tend to last longer than someone whose ministry is more prophetic or evangelistic. Still, we can't plug all the descriptors into a computer and get a divine print-out.

Factors in God's Timing

So how do we decide? Do we discover God's will only on our knees in a quiet office, or does God use other ways to tell us to move on? Does he not frequently indicate his plan through circumstances and then later confirm it with an inner spiritual conviction?

I believe God's will, usually, is the logical thing to do. Therefore, here are some factors I consider when evaluating a possible change.

• *Major problems in the present church.* I don't mean routine snags. You can't run away every time things don't go your way. Problems are challenges to overcome. By handling them, our ministry grows and our relationship with God becomes more precious. One chronic troublemaker in a church usually isn't reason for leaving. Every congregation has its quota of grace-builders, and while it is a delight to leave them behind when you move on, the Lord has prepared more of the same in the next congregation!

But major personality conflicts, congregational dissatisfaction, or tension with a board may mean something more. If I need to take a vote of confidence to know where I stand with the people, chances are it's time to start packing. Taking a vote will likely only divide the people further. I'm already in trouble!

Regardless of who is at fault, persistent problems may be indicators that it is time to seek another pastorate. The church may simply have situations beyond my ability to handle. I'm in over my head. The situation may need someone with ministerial gifts I don't have.

A friend of mine has struggled with this. He's had a successful term as pastor, but things have come unglued lately. He's prepared to leave, but his ego wants to stay and solve the problem so he can go out a winner. He doesn't realize that by staying he's only compounding the difficulties.

God's will became clear in one of our major moves through a situation my wife and I faced. We were overseas in our second missionary term and were excited about the overall task. However, week-to-week functioning was another matter, and I found myself frustrated with decisions and events beyond my control. I saw that this was not a personality problem; it was rather a disagreement about policy.

I was prepared to sacrifice my life but not to waste it. In this setting, God's will became apparent. It was time to cut loose.

While insurmountable problems may be an indicator that it's time to move on, success is no reason to stay. Some have argued that things are going so well it would be wrong to leave. Yet God moved Philip out of Samaria in the middle of a great revival. The absence of problems is no reason to stay put.

• *Ministerial exhaustion.* Every pastorate includes stress. But there are times when we are called to deal with unusually tough situations that tax all our spiritual and emotional strength.

A close friend of mine recently went through such a situation. An adulterous relationship in his church involved a senior board member and a woman from a prominent family. The pastor dealt with them prayerfully and wisely. Innocent parties were protected, hurt spouses were counseled, and the offending parties confronted. But the process of discipline, counseling, and rehabilitation took a year. When it was over, though my friend had performed admirably and had retained the people's confidence, he was emotionally and spiritually drained. There was nothing left to give on Sunday mornings. He needed a fresh start.

Others have felt the same at the end of a building program. The months of worrying and wrangling with contractors, blueprints, and committees have taken a heavy toll. The pastor quietly vows to work smarter next time. He knows he should stay for at least another year and help the congregation cope with its new mortgage. But he is out of gas.

Some young preachers tell their people everything they know in eighteen months. Though they study and search for sermon material, because of their inexperience, they come up with little. To carry on indefinitely can hardly be God's will when additional training or perhaps an assistant pastorate is indicated.

Another variation of this comes simply in the flow of one's ministry and the cycles of a church. One pastor told me recently, "I had completed my major goals and plans. It was time for the church to move on to its next phase of development. I either had to catch a new vision or leave. I chose to leave."

Many pastors are able to sense this. Others can't. Some are such visionaries they will never complete their ideas. For them to wait for the end of a cycle would mean they would never move. Others might not move because they simply don't have the ability to complete their present dreams.

• *Financial pressures.* If a pastor is struggling to keep bread on the table, God may reward faithfulness by raising a new opportunity that will provide for the family. It's time we got off the guilt trip that a move to another church where we will be better cared for is all wrong. We are not in this work for the money. But God does know our needs and takes note of our faithfulness.

• *Family circumstance.* Most of us Protestant clergy face an extra consideration: Our ministry location affects not only ourselves but also our families. The decision to leave a community is a big factor in both the education and social development of our children. Any father, ordained or not, who does not consider the implications of a move for his family is neither loving nor true to the Scripture.

Some of my friends suggest that if it's God's will for you to move, he will take care of your family no matter when or where you go. That is true—if the move is his intention. What some forget, though, is that the social, spiritual, and educational needs of a pastor's family can be an indicator of God's will! God can speak through the needs of a wife or a child as well as through times alone in the prayer closet.

• *Larger opportunity.* First, let me state that the concept of promotion or career advancement is a secular notion and is foreign to the New Testament concept of ministry. There is no spiritual totem pole to climb. God is looking for faithfulness where we are. More than one pastor, however, thinks that if a larger church beckons, it must be a signal that he is God's man of faith and power for the hour. It's not always so.

However, as our ministries mature, God does place us in positions of greater responsibility. As our ability develops to handle larger churches, administer more complexity, and speak to more diverse congregations, God does open up new areas of service. And that frequently means calling in the moving van.

No place of ministry should be belittled. No location is insignificant or deserving of less than a pastor's best. But as our ministry gifts mature, we can become frustrated if there is not a sufficient outlet to release them.

I experienced this in the months prior to one move. Things were going well. The programs I was responsible for were expanding and were well received. There was good rapport with the congregation. But a nagging sense came that God wanted me to use certain ministry gifts that had no present opportunity. I was locked in. This growing spiritual frustration indicated it was time to move on.

Confirmation came one Sunday morning while leading the congregation in worship. No one in the sanctuary was aware of it, but as we sang "He Leadeth Me," the words "By his own hand, he leadeth me . . ." bore special application. It wasn't a human emotion but a divine impression. I knew in that moment that God knew where I was, that he understood my ministry, and that he had a plan for my future. It was just a matter of days until the phone rang with the next invitation.

Hearing God's Voice

After weighing all the factors, there is still one intangible element. It is the most important. We can list all the pros and cons on a sheet of paper (as I have done occasionally), but if we want to function in the pattern of New Testament ministry, we still have to hear God's voice.

It's difficult to explain that subjective conviction. Yet as surely as God's Spirit directed Paul away from Asia and Bithynia but on to Macedonia, so God guides his people today.

I learned this after finishing my theological training. Faced with the choice of beginning pastoral work or furthering my education, I sought counsel from friends and competent leaders. The advice split right down the middle.

That summer I spent a week at a camp counseling teenagers. Little did they know the struggle I was going through. I shared it with no one, but I fasted the main meal each day and spent the time in personal prayer. By Friday, I knew what I should do. There was no bright light flashing. A bird did not come and whisper a divine message in my ear. But there was a burning conviction that I should go back to the university. And there was peace in my spirit.

My mother taught me another good lesson in decision making. Once I had two options to consider. Both were challenging situations and presented exciting possibilities. For some time I couldn't make up my mind. My head said one thing, my heart said another. In talking with my parents, my mother commented, "I don't know what you will do, Cal, but I know you will do the right thing."

At first I brushed it off as the confidence any mother would have in her son. But that wasn't what she meant. She went on to explain, "If your motives are right, and you are prayerful in making the decision, God will not let you make a mistake."

She was right. If you honestly want to move in God's will, he won't let you foul up a decision that affects his church.

That doesn't mean all will turn out glowingly. There may be hard times ahead in the church to which we are sure God sent us. Our ministry may even be rejected there after a while. But we will not be outside the larger channel of God's purpose for our shaping and growth.

Recently, I faced the decision to move again. Several ministerial peers put considerable pressure on me to accept the nomination for a full-time position on the general executive of our Canadian fellowship of churches. The post carries great responsibility, considerable prestige, and challenge. It was tempting. But despite its significance and the urging of others, I turned it down. It wasn't God's time to leave. An inner conviction said I should stay.

Ultimately this is a step of faith. The world calls it biting the bullet. For most of us, it is a difficult time. There is no joy in it, but it is part of God's calling.

At some time prior to entering public ministry, most of us had a confrontation with God. We dealt with self and pride. If we were serious about our faith, we made Jesus our Lord and entered a servant-Master relationship. From that point on, it doesn't matter where we're located geographically. What others think is not important. Personal comfort is secondary. Prestige and large crowds are not determining factors. Loyalty and obedience are. Doing God's will is all that matters.

"The sheep listen to his voice. He calls his own sheep by name and leads them out. When he has brought out all his own, he goes on ahead of them, and his sheep follow him because they know his voice" (John 10:3–4).

This is what determines the time to move. His voice. His will.

T W O

THE WILDERNESS OF THE CANDIDATE

*A good vocation is simply a firm
and constant will in which the
called person has to serve God in
the way and in the places to which
Almighty God has called him.*

FRANCIS DE SALES

Once the decision has been made to move, the external call becomes more preoccupying than the secret call, at least for a short time. Perhaps because of this intrusion, many pitfalls lurk within the candidating process. It's easy to become cynical. Ben Patterson, pastor of Irvine (California) Presbyterian Church, remembers:

"The contrast between my ordination and some of my early candidating was marked. My ordination was an incredible experience. I had been a student who got either A's or F's. I would do something very well, build up everyone's expectations, and then turn around to do something totally irresponsible. Even the people I knew best, who really believed I was called to ministry, were totally befuddled by the way I behaved sometimes. So my ordination was a time for a collective sigh of relief from them—and myself as well.

"But when it came to candidating, I was suspicious of the church. I guess I'd learned it from talking to pastors who told me the organized church had stuck it to them. They were poorly paid and unappreciated. Thus, I went into candidating with a pretty hard-nosed attitude: You're going to pay me right, you're going to give me time off, you're going to recognize my uniqueness, etc. I was terribly protective of myself. So were a lot of my seminary classmates."

Patterson blushes to review those days now, calling himself not only unrealistic but also far from his own view of the high calling.

"The only healthy part of my attitude was that I really wanted the church to know my faults. I had gotten hurt in previous situations when people were surprised by my failings. I didn't want that to happen again. So I had an almost compulsive desire to make sure they knew where I was weak.

"I still feel that way. I bend over backwards to reveal my gaps to candidating committees.

"The dominant feeling in candidating is that you are totally naked. It's one thing to apply for a job, it's another to apply for your calling. If you apply to pump gas, you're not devastated if they turn you down. But when you apply for a church position, it's something you've been preparing all your life to do, and God has called you to it. If they turn you down, what does that mean?"

The only protection Patterson has found is to define candidating as a basic faith issue. It has more to do with God than with the committee, he believes. In this chapter, he explores what that means.

It's a good thing Jesus didn't have to candidate for the position of Messiah.

Being in all points tempted like as we are, however, he faced a comparable situation. He came out of seminary (so to speak) with a mighty flourish, a commencement ceremony at the river Jordan crowned by a Voice from heaven that announced to all gathered relatives, friends, and future parishioners, "This is my son, whom I love; with him I am well pleased." An impressive start.

Then came Satan's design to challenge and undermine everything God had said about Jesus. Had our Lord bought into the alternatives presented, he would have ceased to fulfill his calling.

When a seminary says, "These are our children, whom we certify; with them we are well pleased," it waves farewell to what it firmly believes is the new pastoral leadership of the church. Quickly following or even overlapping this event, however, is another that contrasts sharply. It is the process of candidating . . . the minister's temptation.

And unlike Jesus, most of us have to go through the wilderness more than once as the years of our ministry progress.

Pastor on Parade

The specifics of the process vary from denomination to denomination, but the goal is the same: connect a person with a church, get a job (shanana), fill a position. The temptations are manifold while this is taking place. The minister is usually in a precarious financial situation; funds are low and the future uncharted. Understandably, he wants some kind of security.

Hence, the great temptation of the candidate: to sell himself to the prospective buyer (congregation). As résumés are filled out and interviews are held, the urge to unleash the phantoms of style and image and first impression nudges aside the substance of the candidate. In short, the integrity of God's call and leadership in his life is vitiated, sometimes even eclipsed.

I know of at least one seminary in my denomination that holds special dossier-writing classes for its seniors. Students are cautioned to keep the language vague enough to appeal to as many churches as possible—something very important when just beginning a ministry. You can get more specific about yourself and what you believe later on when you have proved yourself out on the field. The placement office of that same institution has kept a map with little flags stuck into it each time a student lands a job. Sometimes the flags are annotated with who was at that church last and where he or she was able to go from there, the proximity of golf courses to the church office, and other such vital information.

Pastors are no different from anyone else; they are sinners too. When a sinner doesn't know where he is going and is fatigued over where he has been, a spiritual crisis is likely to develop. But there are other reasons for this wilderness, not related to the individual candidate, and much harder to deal with. They have to do with the shape the church has taken in

North American history, all flowing out of the concept of a "free" church.

The Making of Our Wilderness

In his book *The Lively Experiment*, church historian Sidney Mead has written a brilliant essay on the impact of American denominationalism. Something happened here in the early years of this nation that had not happened for more than a thousand years of European church history: the concept of "free" churches became dominant in religious life. No church would be established by the state. No church or governing body would prevent the establishment or spread of any other churches.

The church was to be "free," and with that concept — which was in itself revolutionary — came an even more revolutionary idea. The power of any church could no longer rest on its authority or on coercion. The power of a church came now from its ability to *persuade* its members. Protestant churches in the United States as well as Canada thus became voluntary associations of individuals. The glue that held them together, and still holds them together, is what Mead calls the principle of "voluntaryism." It is the ideology that people should come together independent of civil power and independent of each other, freely giving their consent to submit to the authority of the church. Moreover, consent is not given once for all. It must be won by the church and its leaders again and again.

This is the crucial point to grasp. If leadership in "free" churches comes from the power of persuasion, then whatever else pastors or denominational leaders may be able to do, they *must* be able to persuade, to be politicians.

More than anything I can think of, this explains the preponderance of demagogues and showmen. From the beginnings of our history, we have insisted that our leaders be men of the people. Sometimes that has been good, as in an Abraham

Lincoln or a Dwight L. Moody. But often it has encouraged the likes of those whose names escape me at the moment.

Voluntaryism has also tended to breed mediocrity in church leaders. To lead, they must be tuned in to the people they would lead. Of course, any leader should. The problem is they must be so in touch with the people that they cannot risk being too brilliant or creative or innovative. Otherwise they may be perceived as too removed and too unlike their constituencies, which spells certain death for a leader in the egalitarian, voluntaryistic North American church. When Gerald Ford took office, he told us in a speech that what we were getting was "a Ford, not a Lincoln." I will leave it to historians and political scientists to determine whether or not he delivered on his promise of mediocrity. But I will venture to state that churches generally prefer Fords.

Candidates know all these things and more when they seek positions in churches. Even if they cannot articulate it, they know they have to woo the committee. They sense that if they are successful, they will have to continue to woo the people in order to stay. That bit of realpolitik doesn't render leadership with integrity impossible. It just makes it very difficult, perhaps overwhelmingly so, for many pastors, especially the young.

A Few Remedies

What can we do about this? I don't have many proposals. Perhaps we could learn something from those traditions that place recent seminary graduates according to the decision of a bishop or other ruling body rather than having them candidate. As one Episcopal bishop put it, at least they get the message that they are servants of the Church of Jesus Christ, not this or that particular church—or worst of all, their own career ambitions.

We could also look a little more critically at what our history has meant for us, especially we who have been so profoundly influenced by the "free" church ideology. If we were more aware of the sins endemic to our particular way of doing things, we might be more specific in our prayers for grace to overcome those sins.

That is the issue, is it not, even for us pastoral veterans, who are often worn out, depressed, confused, and facing the dark night of the soul? We are never exempt from the temptation to make our congregations a clientele. We never rise above the urge to twist our calling into a career. Whatever our system or tradition, it cannot save us from our sin. Only Jesus can, and we must repent of our evil ways and believe the gospel every day of our lives.

THREE

A GUIDE
TO CANDIDATING

I cannot recall,
in any of my reading,
a single instance of a prophet
who applied for the job.

A. W. TOZER

Some practical hints can make finding a church easier. Douglas Scott, rector of Saint Martin's Episcopal Church, Radnor, Pennsylvania, has worked out a valuable process for candidating, a process born after several bouts at the only slightly sanctified negotiating table.

"Being in a highly structured church," he says, "I had a lot of help the first time out. I was going to be a shared person between my bishop's staff and a congregation in the Philadelphia area. I got a call one day from someone in the bishop's office saying, 'We're going to get together with you, the bishop, and the rector from the church and hammer out a good working agreement.'

"I went determined to be as tough as George Meany—and ended up saying about two words the whole session. I sat in the corner while my future was thrown onto the table and apportioned between two parties. I felt like a pawn. I never got a chance to say, 'These are my skills, this is my training, these are my gifts.' "

The next time around, Scott was applying for an assistant post.

"This was my first real interview, and like all young clergy, I was excited about finally seeing my gifts and talents appreciated and used. I fully expected to be able to work out the Lord's ministry jointly. What I really found was myself in the middle of a debate about whether

my appearance, politics, and taste in popular music would fit this congregation.

"After several experiences like this, you become a little cynical about the process. I did. And that's why I wrote this chapter on candidating and interviewing. I had heard so many clergy who were embittered by the process. Too many end up feeling like a piece of raw meat. Anyone is allowed to take a slap at the meat to see if it's firm enough to hold up under pressure.

"You're there because after a tremendous amount of training and prayer, the Lord has led you to this place. You quickly find you're one of eighty whom the Lord has led to this place.

"How can the pastor get hold of this process? The pastor needs an edge. Otherwise he or she has a good chance of being semibrutalized, and the ministry demeaned to boot.

"Remember, this is not like applying for a teller's job at a bank. It's different in two ways, one practical, the other spiritual. Practically, when you apply for a teller's position, you talk to one person, maybe two. You quickly get an idea of what the person wants and what the situation calls for. Definite parameters are set. In churches, you walk into a room with as many as thirty-five people; you have little opportunity to find out what joys, hopes, and fears each of them brings to the interview; you're adrift. You don't know what's coming and have no control.

"Spiritually, God is at work in this process, as bad and flawed as it is. I've been to a lot of interviews now, and I'm astounded at how frequently the Spirit surrounds the most difficult of situations.

"I've also learned that the Spirit seems even more real and present if you've done your homework and prayed about the interview."

In the following chapter, Scott outlines what that homework entails.

I took a deep breath to push the fatigue from my mind and body. After traveling seven hours, my wife and I were now holding cups of strong coffee, surrounded by thirty people, and trying to connect names with faces.

They examined us closely, some smiling, some sizing us up like wary customers looking for a used car. Four months of correspondence, telephone conversations, research, and prayer had brought us to this moment. Every facet of my life would soon be explored publicly. I knew I would need the endurance of a distance runner just to withstand this evening. I was being interviewed.

The church, a major congregation in the South, was looking for a senior pastor. They had sent me a bulky package of materials—results of a congregational self-study, membership statistics, a statement of mission and purpose, and comprehensive financial reports for the previous five years.

I, in turn, had provided them with my background and experience.

We had planned our three-day interview trip with surgical precision—the children were with my parents in Philadelphia, the dog housed at a kennel, the airline connections engineered so my absence would not be missed, and other clergy covering for me. It had been expensive and exhausting, but we were excited about the possibilities.

As we moved to our chairs, front and center, I prayed for discernment, knowing our conversations the next three days might well affect the rest of our lives. The chairman stood to begin the discussion.

Looking at me over the tops of his reading glasses, he said, "Before we begin, I want y'all to know I had to live up with Yankees for a year back in 1965, and I didn't like it one bit! What makes you think you're gonna be happy livin' down here?"

My wife and I exchanged glances and knew at once—it was all over.

That interview, at least, left no doubt about the congregation's attitudes—which is better than search committees and candidates performing a verbal dance trying to appear as attractive as possible in the ecclesiastical mating ritual. Often discussion is merely an exchange of theological pleasantries, with the tragic result that congregation and pastor don't really know each other. At best, this means the first year is spent discovering the truth. At worst, such a flawed process makes everyone disillusioned when unexpected attitudes, ideas, and commitments surface only after the pastor arrives.

How can candidates improve the situation? Can the interview itself be a constructive and even enjoyable process?

Yes. Approached carefully, the interview is an effective tool for discerning expectations. The committee may not have thought back further than the former pastor's resignation, and their forward vision may be limited to moving the new one into the manse. They may be mired in the moment, uncertain where they want to go. At *your* interview, you can minister to them, as well as help discern if this invitation is of God, by exploring their history as God's people in a particular place, helping them focus their present concerns and expand their vision of the future.

The Approach

Upon being invited to interview, one of the first things you must make clear is that you'll be asking a number of questions yourself and that you expect your questions to take at least an hour. Set the interview time accordingly.

Do not assume that they expect you to ask questions. I was once the last of six candidates to interview with a particular church, but the first to ask any questions. After our conversation, one committee member said, "We were surprised you had questions about coming here! We assumed our church was so attractive any clergyman would be glad to come. I don't know if you are the right one for us, but you were the only candidate who forced us to think about what kind of minister our church needs."

You will want to raise three types of questions:

1. Questions of *census* try to discover who the congregation is—the talents, interests, and commitments these people bring to church. Questions of census also look beyond the congregation to the area it serves. Does the church draw its members from the surrounding community? Have there been major demographic shifts in the past ten years, and if so, how has the church addressed these shifts? Do these trends indicate future changes? Is housing in the area affordable for young couples? If not, what is the potential for church growth?

2. Every congregation also has particular *issues* you'll need to know about. Some are low-risk, pleasantly discussed questions of theory; others are powder kegs. Is the church inward- or outward-looking? Have changes in worship practice disrupted the congregation? Was there (or is there) any contention over the previous pastor? Have there been theological or practical divisions? Has a building program alienated anyone? Just as questions of census cannot be divorced from the community at large, neither can questions of issues. Has the school district been affected by busing? Is the community racially, economically, and socially integrated? If so, is the

congregation? Are crime rates increasing? Candidates must explore the social context to understand issues within the church.

3. Questions centering on *structures* attempt to discover both the formal and the hidden networks in the congregation. But they also can probe beyond this particular congregation. Are relations with neighboring churches friendly? Has this church been involved with ecumenical worship, educational, or fellowship programs? Are there strong ties between this congregation and the district, presbytery, or diocese? If the congregation is nonaligned, is there an active clergy association in the community for fellowship and support?

The interview is the time for hard and honest statement. If you expect the church to increase your salary by 15 percent every year, this is the time to tell them so. If you will be disappointed by a midweek service of less than 50 percent of the congregation, explain that now!

Why? Congregational expectations of the clergy beyond the written job description (if there is one) are so erratic they are impossible to state accurately. Some parishioners will expect an eighty-hour work week from you; others will want you to spend significant time with your family. The selection committee cannot represent all the congregational expectations, but they will probably suggest trends.

Many clergy bristle when asked if their spouse will accompany them on the interview. Terse statements are frequently made ("You are hiring me, not my wife!"), which, while true, will not endear you to the committee. Personally, I consider my wife a tremendous asset at a job interview. She has the ability to discern attitudes while I am embroiled in answering questions. In addition, she enjoys having the opportunity to meet the individuals involved—after all, she will have to live with them too! However, many wives (or husbands) feel uncomfortable in this situation and may resent being asked. The wisest policy is to tell the committee graciously that your spouse will (or will not) be accompanying you, whichever is your preference.

Before the Committee

As the interview begins, ask if you might begin with prayer if someone else has not already done so. If you are the one to pray, let your prayer speak to the situation; don't try to impress them with your ability at extemporaneous praying. One honest "Lord Jesus, quiet our anxious hearts" will do more than a thousand "we beseech thee of thy gracious favors."

I believe both candidate and committee are best served if the committee asks their questions first. That way, you can modify yours to follow up on issues they have raised. Your agenda includes not only your concerns but also ministering to their needs.

Preface your questions with a statement that some of the answers you seek are matters of fact, but others are matters of feeling, specifically their feelings. As a result, you realize there may be different answers to one question, and you welcome that diversity of opinion.

It is important to have a list of prepared questions based on your understanding of the congregation rather than appearing to ask questions off the cuff. The best kind of spontaneity, someone once said, is the well-planned kind.

While you may be tempted to deal with specific events, statistics, and services, resist the urge to focus on too narrow an area. While there are no perfect "canned" questions for each interview, I would recommend the following approach. Some questions may be useful the way they are; others will need modification depending on the situation.

The primary purpose is to allow committee members to verbalize their attitudes and expectations. You will find it far more helpful to understand their likes and dislikes than their financial condition for the last ten years.

Questions to Ask

Why am I of particular interest to you?
Start with this question. You are not fishing for compliments, but it helps to know if they're excited about you as

their potential pastor. You also need to know why you are of real interest. The answer may surprise you!

I interviewed with one congregation who confessed (after I asked) that they weren't really interested, but the bishop had asked them to contact me, and they felt obliged to do so. Once I knew that, we were able to talk in depth about their particular situation. As a result, they were able to clarify some issues in congregational life they had not seen prior to my visit.

What has been the most significant event in the life of this congregation since you have been a member?

The question serves two purposes. First, you discover what events are significant to them, which helps both you and the committee focus on future expectations. In addition, you see what ministries this congregation considers significant. Do their responses focus on worship activities? Social functions? Outreach programs? Would you characterize any of those events as significant if they happened in your church?

Aside from the upheaval of looking for a new pastor, what has been the most upsetting event in the life of this church?

Unless this congregation is highly unusual, there has probably never been a public opportunity for members to express their frustration, disappointment, and anger. While they may have had plenty of private (and potentially divisive) opportunities, your question allows them to voice their pain openly. It also allows you the luxury of future vision—that is, knowing what is likely to upset them in the years ahead.

In your opinion, what areas of concern need to be addressed by this congregation?

Delightfully nonspecific, this question may be the perfect invitation for a committee member to open an issue that is unresolved or unrecognized. You must, however, be prepared to bring the group back to your agenda should they spend too much time on isolated concerns.

This question once evoked a heated argument within one search committee over a question of property maintenance. When we pursued it further, I discovered fully half the members expected the pastor to mow the church lawn in summer and shovel the snow in winter.

What kinds of things did your former pastor do particularly well?

Certain questions regarding your predecessor are fair territory as long as you refer to him with respect and treat his ministry with courtesy and honor. Your kindness in asking this question will be appreciated. It allows those present to celebrate their former pastor in a specific way—by holding up his or her particular gifts in ministry. It also allows you to see what aspects of ministry were well received, including tasks that may be expected of you.

What were the circumstances surrounding your former pastor's departure?

You may already know the answer, having heard through the grapevine. But unless the former pastor died in office, it is a good idea to ask so the committee can state the reasons openly. If your predecessor did die in office, or if he was extremely popular and moved on to another congregation, you will have to be sensitive to their need to mourn his departure. If you are following an individual who had a long term as pastor, you may want to ask if the committee feels another long-term pastorate is feasible considering the tenure of your predecessor.

In what areas did you wish your former pastors had more expertise?

"We've had three preachers in a row in this church, and now we need a money man!" Listening to this response by a committee member a few years ago, I felt glad I had asked!

You have cushioned this question by making the subject plural, thus taking the onus off your predecessor, but you've still allowed them to express their opinions about unaddressed areas of need.

Two caveats should be issued: First, you are not talking about personality traits but ministerial skills. Second, ask them to speak only about firsthand experience. Rumors that Pastor So-and-so didn't deal with poor Mr. Jones's suicide very well may be nothing more than that—rumors, and are therefore counterproductive.

What formal and informal methods of support have you used in the past to help your pastor become a better minister?

The question may stop them cold! If they display signs of confusion, offer explanations based on your expectations of congregational support. Did they encourage (and offer to pay for) any continuing education? Are there formal structures to assist the pastor in preaching by providing disciplined feedback? Has the congregation developed methods to evaluate their own performance as Christian ministers?

Tell me about the governing board.

And I mean everything! How are they elected? How frequently? Does the board rotate membership on a regular basis? What is the background, business, and interest of each member? What kind of jobs do they hold? Are they employers or employees? (The answer makes a significant difference in how they treat their clergy!)

Who runs the stewardship, Christian education, youth, mission, and outreach programs? Who oversees building maintenance? Is the church board bound to any state laws in addition to congregational bylaws and denominational methods of procedure? If there is a staff in addition to the pastor, who is responsible for church-staff relations? How much authority does the board exercise in staff management? How frequently does the board meet? How long, on the average, do the meetings last?

The church building may be beautiful, the community ideal, the manse a mansion, but the quality of your working life will be determined largely by your relationship with the board. Discover as much as you can about its members and how they function before you consider accepting this call.

Has the pastor's family traditionally taken an active role in this church?

In answering this question, committee members may reveal how they felt about the level of activity of previous pastors' families. Therein lies the key to the criteria by which your family will be judged.

How is the pastor's compensation package determined? How frequently is it reviewed? By whom? What factors are used in determining that package? Merit or cost-of-living increases? Social Security reimbursement? Equity in the parsonage or a cash equity allowance? Continuing education, book, and automobile allowances?

Presumably, you already know what salary the church is offering. What you are interested in is whether you will be a participant in your salary review a year after your call. You also need to sensitize the committee to the increasing financial burden placed on clergy by factors beyond their control such as Social Security increases (soon to be 13 percent) and the loss of equity by living in church-owned housing.

Far too often, humility (or embarrassment) prevents clergy from honestly discussing financial needs, but the laborer is worthy of his hire, and your compensation package must meet the needs of your family. Your interest in the process and participation in annual reviews must be stated at the outset.

How should your pastor spend his time? In the course of a week, how much time should be spent in prayer? Personal study? Sermon preparation? Administration? Individual and family counseling? Visiting? With the family?

At some point, get specific information about their expectations of your time. I remember asking a question about the rector's personal time, and a vestryman responded, "Day off? Why, our rectors never take a day off!" I accepted the call to that church and found the man wasn't kidding—they fully expected their rector to be available at a moment's notice. It took two years before they became accustomed to my practice of leaving town a day and a half each week.

How many hours do they expect you to work in a week? If you expect to work forty, and they expect eighty, better to know it now! How are those hours to be used? When they are used up and work remains undone, what happens? If you work extra hours one week, will they allow you to take those hours for yourself and your family next week? Do they see prayer, study, and sermon preparation as part of your work week, or things to be done on top of forty hours of hospital and home visiting?

In your questioning, you must not sound judgmental—you are acquiring information. They may have thought of the pastor's job only in the most general terms. These questions force them to state their expectations clearly both for themselves and the candidate.

What organizations in the congregation are the most active or successful?

This allows you to determine the congregational priorities. If the Ladies' Bridge Club is thriving but the Young People's Fellowship is limping along, you know where the interest and commitment is. Ask if any organizations have dissolved in the last two years. If so, why?

Beyond calling a pastor and its related concerns, what is the highest congregational priority for the next twelve months?

Whatever the responses (and there are bound to be more than one), they will form your expected agenda for the next year. You must determine if their interests align with your own. You may want to build a men's program or start an emergency food cupboard, but they may want to panel the church lounge or pave the parking lot.

What goals have you established for church growth? What methods can be used to achieve those goals?

The question of growth is a census question. Where will the new people come from? If this community is like most others, the question will be how to attract and sustain the unchurched. Is the church ready for that?

Perhaps the most honest response I ever received to this question came from one committee member who said, "Getting more people is your job, and I don't care how you do it. I just come here to worship."

While undoubtedly many people feel this way, if that attitude is embraced by the congregation as a whole, the task before you is formidable.

What plans have you made for the expansion of staff or plant?

If they haven't planned for expansion, they don't intend to grow. The vision of their future ministry is bound by the limitations of the present moment. While this may not deter you from accepting the position, you must realize you have some hard work cut out for you, beginning with an expansion of their horizons.

How stable is this congregation financially?

With the recent economic uncertainties, few churches have been able to work toward future financial security. Ask them to speculate aloud about the future financial needs of the congregation.

What programs have you planned to implement in the next ten years?

Many churches feel any plans they may have had go out the window when a new pastor comes. On the other hand, some congregations may be anxious to implement changes the former pastor disallowed. The question allows them to state their dreams of the future. You, in turn, can give them an honest assessment of your interest in those particular programs with relatively little risk.

But How Do I Know?

The search for the perfect congregation is futile. No church can ever fully meet a minister's needs, any more than one minister can fulfill all the expectations of a congregation. Even so, you need not accept every offer that comes along. How do you know when to pursue an interview to the next stage, or to accept the call if offered?

Accepting a call is at best a series of tradeoffs. Are you willing to live with this particular drawback in order to acquire that specific benefit?

Consequently, *before* you begin the process, take time to

assess your professional needs and your family's social and economic needs. What are the nonnegotiables? What are things you'd be willing to wait two years for? What are mere preferences?

Do you have skills as a teacher that you need to use? Are you particularly gifted in youth work? Do you hunger to share your spiritual journey with a group of fellow pilgrims? What family needs will shape your decision? Will your spouse expect or need to work? What stage have your children reached in their schooling? Will their gifts or needs require specialized instruction or guidance?

Don't forget to list areas where you will require assistance. Do you find administrative work a burden and hope to have members of the congregation share the load? Do you depend on lay assistance in visitation? Do you need structured feedback to help you gauge your performance?

An honest assessment of needs will highlight specific areas your interview must address. If your needs assessment is carefully done, you'll know what you require and what you're willing to trade off.

The criteria you establish, however, may not be your final basis for deciding. I once interviewed with a church that presented me with a dozen reasons to say no. Some members of the search committee were guarded, others hostile. Several questions I asked received an answer I didn't expect (or want). Accepting the call would have meant taking a cut in salary and moving my wife and children even farther from our already distant families. I was certain the pastor who accepted this call would be faced with a long list of difficulties.

But I accepted that call nonetheless, convinced that even though it seemed all wrong, it was definitely right.

The interview, stressful and upsetting as it may be, is the best forum for hammering out concerns, commitments, and priorities in an atmosphere of intense excitement and high expectation. Handled carefully and prayerfully, it can be a time of joyous discovery that leads to a long and fruitful relationship.

STARTING OUT AND STAYING IN

*The test of a vocation
is the love of the drudgery
it involves.*

LOGAN PEARSALL SMITH

As a new pastor enters a church, several issues need to be resolved. Some are congregational: questions of authority, trust, and ministry style, for example. These important issues will be discussed in chapters five, six, and seven.

Other issues, however, reside in the psyche of the new pastor. They stem from questions we ask ourselves, such as "Who am I? What am I called to do? Can I really be a pastor?"

Douglas Rumford, pastor of First Presbyterian Church of Fairfield, Connecticut, wrote the following chapter shortly before going to a new church. "It was a break point in my own life, and the process of writing this worked to my advantage. Since that time, I've come to believe that these are issues not just for young pastors, although their needs in these areas may be more acute. It's something we need to face every time we change ministries.

"I shared the article with my Session as we talked about the job to be done at this church. I said, 'Here's who I am,' and we spent an evening talking about it.

"They appreciated it. One man said, 'We never really thought we would intimidate you, but we're glad to know so we can work to

avoid doing it. And it never occurred to us that you might feel inadequate.' "

The following chapter probes the internal issues that hold the power to make or break the beginning pastor in a church, whether this is his first parish or tenth.

I've sometimes wished I could hibernate for about ten years and emerge as a more mature, experienced pastor. While our culture idolizes youth, most churches also desire the wisdom and experience of age. The perfect pastor is thirty-five with at least twenty-five years of experience!

Age and experience are, of course, significant in many careers, but the ministry possesses an age dynamic different from other professions. Young pastors are immediately thrust into positions of leading people their parents' and grandparents' age.

In my second year out of seminary, I was invited to speak at a church renewal weekend. After my first message Friday night, an eighty-two-year-old member told my wife, "When I saw how young he was, I was sure he wouldn't have anything to say to me. Fortunately, I was wrong." When my wife relayed the message to me, I winced because I understood her initial impression. After all, what right *do* I have to teach a person nearly three times my age?

Three primary issues challenge the young pastor's self-concept from the start: idealism, inadequacies, and intimidation. How we respond will do much to set the tone for future ministry.

The Test of Idealism

"My idealism was shot the first week I arrived at this church," one friend told me. A trustee had taken him aside his first Sunday and said, "I'm sure you have great ideas for things to do here, but most of the people will be happy if you just stick to preaching."

Graduates leave seminary and Bible college ready to change the world. They carry a pocketful of programs to lay on some unsuspecting congregation. Visions of superchurches dance in their heads. All this is fine. In fact, this energy and motivation fuel the engines necessary for ministry start-up. J. I. Packer once said, "A task without a vision is drudgery; a task with vision is ministry."

But how does the congregation view a pastor's idealism? Much depends not so much on the ideas themselves as the tone with which they're presented. If the people sense condescension—"Have I got a plan for you!"—they'll likely reject the plan.

A congregation is really asking the pastor, "Do you understand us?" They want to see that the pastor truly knows them and is seeking their best interests. They won't simply sign up for the pastor's ego trip.

Another concern is the cost. Congregations want to know if these plans and their implications have been clearly thought through. They realize they may be left with a half-built program tower that can't be completed.

Whether a congregation responds with outright rejection or the subtle frustrations of heel-dragging, the new pastor's ideals will be challenged. This is natural, and this realization alone can be a comfort. Nevertheless, the wrong reactions to this testing time can undermine effective ministry.

One negative response is resentment. The lack of receptivity can breed impatience and a spirit of accusation. In *Life*

Together, Bonhoeffer counters this attitude: "A pastor should not complain about his congregation, certainly never to other people, but also not to God. A congregation has not been entrusted to him in order that he should become its accuser before God and men."

A second negative response is shifting the accusing gaze from the congregation to yourself. Unrealized ideals may germinate seeds of disillusionment. Initiative erodes. The call is questioned. The pastor is tormented with doubts: *Am I doing enough? Is this really where I belong? Am I being wasted here?* The choice seems to be between forsaking the vision or moving on in search of a more fertile field.

But there's another alternative: refashion the vision. Shared vision involves lots of time, study, and discussion. The foundation must be laid. One pastor came to a church and within his first year proposed they begin the Bethel Bible series for adult education. The congregation thought differently. The defeat hurt, but he took a different approach. He began to whet their appetites for Bible study through small groups and short Bible courses. Three years later, they eagerly entered the Bethel program.

The joy comes from seeking God's will together. We learn from each other. One of our elders said to me recently, "I began to get more excited about my church work when I realized you ministers didn't have a corner on the market of God's will."

The Exposure of Inadequacies

The weaknesses of even the most capable pastors are exposed on the barren heights of ministry. How can I call these people to prayer when my own prayer life is so erratic? How can I expect to lead God's people when I can't control my anger? I can hardly balance my own checkbook; how am I supposed to understand the church budget? Where will I ever get the wisdom for these counseling problems? What do I do when I run out of good sermon ideas?

Soon the realization dawns: the ministry *is* an impossible task. The magnitude of the responsibility is staggering—to minister to the spiritual, intellectual, social, and emotional needs of people of all ages, in all stages of spiritual development. Eternity hangs in the balance.

In the plan of God, realizing our inadequacy is actually the stepping stone to effective ministry. We remain mired in discouragement only until we realize we *are* inadequate and *always will be.* God planned it that way! Feelings of inadequacy loosen their chilling grip when we see that they are actually messengers of God's grace. In *The Person Reborn,* Paul Tournier writes, "In this world, our task is not so much to avoid mistakes, as to be fruitful. To be more and more able to recognize our faults, so as to be better able to understand the price of God's mercy, and to devote ourselves more completely to him, makes our lives more fertile. . . . Our vocation is, I believe, to build good out of evil. For if we try to build good out of good, we are in danger of running out of raw material."

The glory of God is his use of frail, earthen vessels to bear eternal treasures.

A friend of mine became senior pastor of a 600-member church at the age of thirty. In spite of his outward success, he was plagued daily by feelings of inadequacy. As he prayed about this, he felt led to call two of his lay leaders. When they arrived, he said, "I'd like you to lay hands on me and pray for my healing."

They were somewhat taken aback. "Pray for your healing? Why? What's wrong?"

"I'm shattered by a feeling of inadequacy." He went on to describe how this feeling focused his attention on himself. It robbed him of all freedom and confidence in the Lord.

"When they laid hands on me," he said sometime later, "I was healed of my feeling—but not of my inadequacy itself! My inadequacy is a fact; we're all inadequate. But God released me from my fears and discouragement to be a servant to the body of Christ."

In addition to stimulating dependence on God, our inadequacy also calls us to rely on others. As much as pastors may preach on community, it will not happen without interdependence. And interdependence cannot happen without the disclosure of weakness and need. The pastor-on-the-pedestal ends right here.

We admire successful people, but we don't feel close to them unless we know about their struggles. Perfection, real or perceived, imposes distance; weakness unites. Someone said, "The only nice thing about being imperfect is the joy it brings to others." Beyond the cynicism, there's a profound truth: when we admit our inadequacy, it helps forge a mutual ministry between pastor and people. Far from being a curse, openness about our shortcomings can strengthen all involved. We can call forth others' gifts to compensate for our weakness.

The Threat of Intimidation

A young pastor can feel intimidated by the pillars of the church—the large givers, the successful professionals, any number of people. Few young pastors are paralyzed by intimidation, but there's usually one group or person the pastor perceives as a threat to his leadership. Often these thoughts aren't rational. But neither is intimidation. Evidently, Timothy struggled with this. Paul wrote, "Don't let anyone look down on you because you are young" (1 Tim. 4:12). The greatest danger of intimidation is that we begin to devalue ourselves.

To compensate, some young pastors (and some experienced pastors) use distance. They become formal and careful to "follow the book" so there's no risk or cause for accusation. Others respond with drive. They turn on the bravado and forge ahead with great shows of confidence. Others respond with reluctance to take up God's call. We see this reticence in Jeremiah. When God called him, he cried out, "Ah, Sovereign Lord, I do not know how to speak; I am only a child" (Jer. 1:6). But the critical factor in God's eye isn't chronology, it's call.

Our identity in Christ is our greatest asset. When we let go of defensiveness, we can enjoy the freedom of accepting ourselves and others and building a partnership with the people of God.

Rob is a sixty-two-year-old businessman in our congregation who I always felt was antagonistic. During my sermons he would sit with arms folded and brow wrinkled. He seemed to be saying, *I dare you to say something to me.*

After about a year, he seemed to soften. Following a service he said to me, "I think you have what it takes to be a preacher. I'd love to hear you in twenty years." I could only think, *Do I write off my preaching for the next nineteen years?*

Then last Christmas I received a note from Rob in response to a sermon I preached on peace. He wrote:

At age sixty-two, I've probably got at least thirty-five years on you, and time and circumstances have had a better chance at me. So I was pleasantly surprised to listen to your sermon and application of John 14:27.

I'll not be around when you reach age sixty-two, but if I could, it would be interesting to hear you preach again on this verse. You'll probably say about the same thing, but with pauses as you remember all that has happened in your life, and those you have known and loved—and what peace they have found in this life.

Rob has taught me much. He has shown me the need to consider the depth and breadth of experience in the people I serve. "You'll probably say the same thing, but with pauses"—what a profound insight into the meaning of maturity. The firmly believed but quickly spoken words of youth will grow weightier and fuller as we experience God's faithfulness over the years. It will be time to slow down and savor his grace.

Youth is something we all outgrow—much to the regret of many. Personally, rather than fight the fact of age, I want to enjoy the process of maturing daily in Christ. I don't expect the problems of idealism, inadequacy, and intimidation to disappear with the passing of time; they'll just change clothes. One principle remains: when God calls, we dare not let youth, or age for that matter, be a barrier. There's no time to hibernate, only time to grow.

WHO WORKS FOR WHOM?

*The essence of the minister
lies in what God has created
him to be rather than in
what the church authorized him to do.*

JOHN STACEY

The real work of adjusting to a new church begins after the candidating, after the hiring, and after the moving. By this time the church should know what it is getting in its new leader. The résumé tells what he or she can do. The interview may give some indication of how well he thinks on his feet. His comments about expectations and fears reveal something of his humanity and call. But only in the day-to-day shoulder-rubbing of ministry do the true dynamics of working together surface.

One of the most crucial testing grounds is deciding the question of authority. Who is in charge here? And how does that authority work in practice?

Ironically, structure and polity rarely decide this issue. In the business world, the question of who reports to whom pretty well settles the question. In the church, however, the organizational chart rarely reflects true power bases; the pastor is left to operate the best he can, given the realities of tradition, hidden agendas, and personal networks.

Just how does a new pastor settle the question of power in an organization that shuns it? Norman Shawchuck wrote this chapter based on his own pastoral experience in several United Methodist churches and his many years of church consulting work. He has viewed literally hundreds of churches where the power question has been asked and answered in scores of different ways.

If this question is not answered quickly, the new ministry will sputter and stall until a strategy is developed.

One of the most difficult and perplexing tasks for many pastors is confronting a volunteer or part-time worker. The worker may be doing a poor job but happens to be a church member. The pastor is not sure which way the lines of accountability run. Do these people work for him? Or does he work for them?

I know of a church which employs members on a part-time basis for typing, printing, cleaning, and visitation. The office area is crowded and poorly arranged. Several years ago the board gave the pastor permission to make necessary changes. He went to work on the problem by hiring an architect to design a new office arrangement.

Yet to date, no changes have been made. The workers continue to labor in cramped and inefficient conditions. The reason? The architect's design called for moving the printing room. However, the part-time printer, a member of the church, declared he would quit the job and withdraw his membership if the change were made. So the printing machine continues to clack away a few feet from the secretary's desk, and visitors continue to step around and over boxes on their way to the pastor's study.

The pastor allows this to continue because he is not sure of his authority when it involves a part-time employee who is also a church member. Is the pastor accountable to the employee as a member, or is it the reverse?

As a young pastor I served a small church in which the Sunday school superintendent was the wife of the board chairman. The Sunday school hour was the first event of the day, and this family was consistently fifteen minutes late. Sunday after Sunday I would do a slow burn while the congregation impatiently waited for her to arrive to conduct the opening exercises.

On several occasions I tried to move the starting time back fifteen minutes, but the board, led by the chairman, consistently refused. This situation continued for about two and a half years, until finally in desperation I stood up at the exact minute Sunday school was scheduled to begin and asked the people to go immediately to their classrooms. I waited in the auditorium.

True to form, fifteen minutes later the Sunday school superintendent and her husband arrived. There were angry words. She resigned. I survived the ordeal.

Why had I allowed this one person to frustrate an entire Sunday school operation so long before taking action? I was never sure of my authority to correct the situation. I knew I was somehow responsible for the Sunday school program, yet this woman and her husband were church members. They had voted on my coming to the church. They helped pay my salary by their contributions. She had been elected to her position at a congregational meeting.

These scenarios are not unique. As a consultant for church organizations, I talk almost every week with at least one pastor who is having problems with a volunteer or paid worker and feels helpless to correct the situation.

Authority-accountability issues are rooted in the very nature of the church as a voluntary organization. This makes it nearly impossible to establish direct-line accountability structures, and the diffusion of power tends to weaken all positions of authority.

Lack of Direct-Line Accountability

In a corporation, a boss sits at the top of a hierarchical pyramid with the authority to establish and enforce an accountability structure, a chain of command. The local church is usually an association of volunteers. There is no boss at the top with workers filling their dutiful place beneath him or her.

The church is comprised of individual members who individually feel ownership of the organization. This personal and widespread sense of ownership raises the primary question: Who actually has the authority to make final decisions? Who is the boss? Often the volunteer worker feels he or she is a final decision maker since he or she shares in the "ownership" of the organization as a member and contributes time and money.

Though the pastor accepts a salary from the members, he may not consider himself their employee, since his qualifications and ordination into ministry were not determined by them. Also, the responsibilities of the pastor are much more like those of the chief executive officer of an organization than those of a rank-and-file employee.

In a denominational hierarchy, a pastor finds officials (bishops, superintendents, etc.) who often consider themselves to be final decision makers. The pastor's position is further complicated by the fact that he is the liaison between the church and the denomination's governing body. Whose interests, goals, and programs does he pursue when the interests of the local church conflict with the governing body's?

For example, most denominations attempt to finance their regional and national offices through some form of assessment upon local churches, who often resent and oppose these financial demands. They feel they have too little to say about how the money is spent, or simply want to keep the money for their local-church programs.

The pastor finds himself caught between the desires of the governing body and the local church. The local church expects the pastor to support its position, since he "works for the congregation." The denominational board expects the pastor to support its position, since he is its "chief representative on the local level." Each side is capable of creating considerable pressure.

For example, the local church often uses financial demands placed upon it by the denomination as a reason for not increasing the pastor's salary or underwriting programs the pastor supports. The denomination board often uses the church's level of giving to denominational causes as one criterion when considering the pastor's qualification for serving a larger or more prestigious church. Through its actions the local church communicates to the pastor, *If you fail to support our position that we should pay a smaller assessment, we may take the money from your salary.* The governing board, however, communicates, *If you do not see to it that your church pays its full amount, we may recommend or appoint you to less-than-desirable churches.*

In almost every instance, both the local church and the denominational board lack sufficient authority over the pastor to absolutely force their will. No one is really certain to whom the pastor is actually accountable, the congregation or the denomination. Because of this fuzzy accountability structure, the pastor often develops a major allegiance to his own sense of integrity—an accountability that overrides all others. The pastor becomes a Lone Ranger. Pressured to support everyone, he becomes accountable to no one.

By Lone Ranger leaders, I refer to those who believe their own ideas are usually best, their solutions to problems are the most workable, and their program interests are closest to the mind of God. In short, they assume they know what is best for the church, and so it seems appropriate to make unilateral decisions and do whatever is necessary to persuade the congregation to accept such decisions.

I recently conducted a pastors' workshop dealing with how to develop communication and training processes that keep the laity fully informed and involved in the affairs of the church. A young pastor (two years out of seminary) was visibly shaken by the concepts being discussed and finally jumped to his feet and said, "I want to keep my congregation ignorant and passive. That is the only way I can be sure of maintaining control." He had already felt the pressure and had become a Lone Ranger. He wanted the freedom to ride in whatever direction he thought was best. He had learned that if the congregation played the part of Tonto, they would be more likely to follow his leading and support his programs.

Another common example is a pastor who begins his ministry by dismantling the programs started by a former pastor. Isn't it interesting that so many pastors seem to know what is better for the church than the pastor who preceded them? Isn't it also interesting that these same pastors often criticize their own predecessors for behaving in a similar manner? Such are the effects of succumbing to a Lone Ranger style of leadership.

The Diffusion of Power

As previously stated, in a corporation power tends to revolve around the boss at the top. The boss releases small amounts of power and allows it to trickle down through the structure. This approach never relinquishes final authority. It remains vested in the boss. He delegates certain powers to his immediate subordinates, and they are fully accountable. They in turn hold their subordinates accountable for certain powers and responsibilities. Thus responsibility and accountability are established throughout the organization with all persons being ultimately accountable to the top executive, and dependent upon him for the necessary power to carry out their responsibilities.

Remember that the local church is an association of volunteers "owned" by all the members, and each feels he possesses a portion of the decision-making power. They do not perceive a single boss sitting at the top from which power and authority originate. Rather, these originate at the grassroots of the entire membership base. The members, each one, can choose to share power with leaders and programs they like or to withhold it from leaders and programs they do not like. The members see themselves as bosses and the pastor as a power broker who collects power from individuals and channels it into programs and ministries the members like well enough not to withdraw their power. Thus the pastor must gain and keep the trust and support of enough members to "borrow" sufficient power to lead.

An example of the pastor as power broker can be seen in a church I recently visited. The parsonage was old and in need of major repair. The trustees decided it would be best to dispose of the old property and purchase a different one. The congregation approved, though there was minority opposition.

When the trustees decided to purchase a home requiring about four thousand dollars in remodeling costs, the minority opposition became very vocal, claiming the trustees should have purchased a home requiring no costs beyond the purchase price. Some members stopped contributing to the church budget. Others threatened to leave the church altogether.

For several months the parsonage project and many ministry programs limped along, while the congregation struggled with the limits of trustee authority, endeavoring to appease all sides. In all of this, the pastor remained neutral.

Finally, in a congregational meeting I attended, the pastor clearly stated the positions of the opposing groups and asked for questions and answers. He implored people to forgive one another and urged all members to support the trustees' decision. At that point, several members who had also remained neutral in the conflict said they supported the pastor's position. After hearing several such statements, one of the opposing members said she too would support the pastor's position. Another member of the neutral group immediately contributed four thousand dollars to cover the remodeling costs. The issue that had paralyzed the congregation for several months was over in a few minutes, and with a happy ending!

How was this possible? Enough members sufficiently trusted the pastor to lend their power to his position once he made it known. In this instance, that power came from neutral persons who moved to the support of the pastor, a leader of the opposing group who reversed her position, and a neutral member who contributed the money. The turning point was the power broker position of the pastor.

This example forcefully illustrates that power owned by members is comprised of their ability to support or to oppose, to attend or to stay away, to volunteer or refuse to serve, to contribute finances or to withhold. The ultimate display of the member's ability to withdraw his or her portion of the power is the closed purse and the empty pew. *The member who never attends and/or never contributes is exercising tremendous power.* The member who loudly opposes the pastor and program at committee meetings, who causes many frustrations and headaches, is not exercising nearly as much negative power as the disappointed, nonsupportive member who closes his or her purse and goes silently away. Few church leaders realize this.

Local-church power is a diffuse entity. Much of it rests with volunteers (members) whom the pastor can direct and lead only as they are willing to be led. To lead effectively, the pastor must be empowered by the very persons he is to lead.

Are There Solutions?

While the lack of direct-line accountability and the diffusion of power in the local church can create a lot of problems, it is certainly not all bad. This situation creates a climate in which laity and clergy alike can enjoy a great deal of individual freedom. From this freedom can come creativity and opportunity to involve many members in the ministries of the church.

Most breakdowns occur because of a lack of understanding the expectations and a pervasive sense of powerlessness to influence decisions. In my parish consulting work, I've found four areas of breakdown that can occur in any congregation regardless of size, location, or theology. They are:

1. The lack of establishing a clear and unique purpose for the church and each of its program units;

2. The lack of recruiting leaders who have the ability to fulfill those purposes;

3. The lack of developing a ministry covenant with each leader that spells out expectations of the task;

4. The lack of teaching and modeling good leadership principles.

After the painful experience with the Sunday school superintendent in my first parish, I was determined never again to allow such situations to develop and fester. In the next parish, I began my preaching by stressing that the congregation had a distinct and unique mission to perform (every congregation does), and it was our responsibility before God to discover and fulfill that mission. Mission is what God calls each congregation to be and do at a particular point in its history. My messages focused upon questions such as "For what reason did God bring us together as a congregation at this particular time, in this particular community? What are we to be and do that no other congregation in town, or in our denomination, could be or do?"

While stressing the mission of the entire church, I also requested the board to research the unique mission of our church in light of personal needs in the congregation, needs of the community that our church could and should do something about, and how our church could and should support the mission of our denomination. The result was a *statement of mission* that was presented to the congregation for discussion and adoption.

The mission statement was then given to *each program committee in the church* with the request they respond to the following questions aimed at clarifying the unique purpose of their particular ministry:

1. *What is the unique purpose of our committee? What are we*

called to be and do that is distinct and different from all other committees in the church?

2. *What important aspects of the church's program will be left
undone if we do not do them?*

3. *How does our purpose support the congregation's mission
statement?*

4. *Specifically, what skills, knowledge, and attitudes do we have
or must we develop in order to fulfill our purpose as we have described
it?*

The material generated by each committee was presented
to the board, who reviewed it from the following perspectives:

1. *Are there gaps in our total ministry? Are important areas or
activities not being covered by any program committee?*

2. *Are there overlaps? Should any ministry area or activity be
covered by more than one committee?*

3. *What adjustments are necessary in any of these purpose statements to close a gap, reduce an overlap, and assure that if every
committee accomplishes its purpose, the congregation's mission will
be satisfactorily fulfilled?*

4. *What additional skill, knowledge, and attitudes do we suggest
for any particular program?*

This process took about five months to complete. The final
results were reported to the congregation and the program
committees with the request that they begin to formulate
specific plans to accomplish their purpose. Now I was to learn
that there are traditions and policies in a local church that
stand ready to challenge any effort to develop accountability
on the part of its workers.

Seven months remained before the annual congregational
meeting, which would elect new officers and workers. I called
a meeting of the nominations and personnel committee. The
first question raised was "Why are we meeting so far ahead of
time?" This led to an interesting discussion in which I learned
some things:

1. The nominating committee "traditionally" met only
twice a year. Both meetings were held during the month
preceding the annual meeting.

2. Generally, four or five inactive members were nominated to leadership positions as a means of inducing them to begin attending church.

3. Persons to be nominated were not contacted prior to the annual meeting to discover whether they had sufficient time or interest to do the job well.

4. The nominations were kept secret until the annual meeting, at which time nominations were allowed from the floor. Two or three "nominees" would usually withdraw their names. Generally, however, elections would be made according to the slate prepared by the nominating committee.

I explained that the reason for calling an early meeting was because the committee's work was so important it could not be done in a couple of meetings. I described their suggested work as follows:

I. Prepare a description of each leadership position in the church.

   A. Define the purpose of the program for which leadership will be offered. (Most of this was done in the earlier work of the program committees and the board.)

   B. List the tasks and responsibilities the person is to fulfill.

   C. Outline the necessary skills, knowledge, and attitudes.

   D. Estimate realistically the time required to do the task well.

   E. Suggest ways training could be provided if the person being recruited does not possess the necessary skills and knowledge.

This information would be prepared as a Ministry Covenant that included places for the signatures of the person who would finally accept the task and the board's chairperson.

II. Conduct a leadership study of the entire church in terms of positions held, quality of performance, skills, and knowledge. Also list work areas of possible interest for future service.

III. Recruit a qualified person to fill each position. Ask:
   A. Does this person have the ability to do the job well?
   B. Does this person have sufficient time to give to the job?
   C. Does this person have sufficient interest in the job?
IV. Visit the person to be recruited at least two times. The first visit is to review the job description and ascertain a possible interest. The second visit is to obtain a response for filling the position. Training should be discussed during both visits.
V. Present to the annual meeting only those names of persons who have indicated a willingness to serve and who have signed a Ministry Covenant.

By signing the covenant, the person would agree to fulfill the expectations of the task. The signature of the board's chairperson would pledge the church to provide the necessary resources and training to do the job well and with a sense of personal satisfaction.

The committee worked long and hard to complete their task two weeks before the annual meeting. The slate of nominees was distributed to the entire congregation with a full description of the process the committee had followed. The election process at the annual meeting proved to be *pro forma*. The following Sunday morning we commissioned all the workers and presented each one with a framed copy of his or her Ministry Covenant.

The work of the nominations and personnel committee was not finished with the commissioning service. They immediately went to work implementing the training of those who had agreed to serve. The committee also developed a performance review procedure to discuss periodically the following with the workers:

1. Whether the program was accomplishing its purpose.

2. Whether the worker was keeping his or her ministry covenant.

3. Whether additional resources and/or training were needed to do the task well.

An interesting situation developed while the nominations and personnel committee was conducting the leadership study. It became apparent that the person holding the position of lay delegate to the denomination's annual business session had been elected to that position for the past five years but had not attended a single session. We agreed this person would be nominated again only if she signed the Ministry Covenant.

During the committee's first and second visits, she said she definitely wanted the job and expected to be nominated; but "because no one can predict the future," she would not sign the covenant. The committee still voiced strong opinion that she should be nominated. After much discussion I learned a bit more about traditions in this church.

Over the years this woman had always indicated which job she wanted and was given it even though no one could remember a time she had performed the task. Some previous nominating committees had attempted to correct the situation by not nominating her. However, each time her husband had entered her name at the annual meeting along with personal threats against the pastor as well as a threat to leave the church if she were not elected. Every time, the congregation had elected her over the names suggested by the committee. After much discussion, the committee decided it could not in good conscience nominate her.

Her name did not appear on the slate of nominees distributed to the congregation two weeks before the annual meeting. True to form, her husband visited me. Threats were made. He also visited members of the committee to tell them of the threats. There was another committee meeting and a reaffirmation of its decision to nominate no one who had not signed a Ministry Covenant.

At the annual meeting, her husband entered her name in nomination for the position. The committee chairperson then reminded the congregation of the process it had followed, saying, "This person has been visited but has declined to sign the Ministry Covenant." She received two votes.

Her husband demanded a meeting with the board and the denomination's district superintendent. We agreed, and declared the meeting open to all who wished to attend. One week later the auditorium was filled for the meeting!

The district superintendent asked why the meeting had been called. The husband gave his version of the election, said the pastor was "trying to run the whole show," and demanded that the district superintendent appoint me to another church. There was instant bedlam, with members standing throughout the auditorium shouting for the floor.

After the district superintendent gained control of the meeting, we heard members one by one affirm the process the nominating committee had used. The district superintendent asked whether anyone cared to speak in opposition to the process or the results of the election. There was not one dissenting statement. We as a nominating committee and pastor had faced a powerful challenge. Members of the congregation had sufficiently trusted the process to loan us the necessary power to survive the challenge.

By the time the meeting was over, I knew we had succeeded in establishing new norms of accountability, even in a church where direct-line accountability structures were not possible. By the way, the couple *did not* leave the church, and in the following years both became active, faithful workers.

SIX

BUILDING TRUST

*We ought not to make
any conditions of our
brethren's acceptance with
us but such as God has
made the conditions of
their acceptance with him.*

MATTHEW HENRY

The question of authority cannot finally be settled, though, until another issue is resolved: trust. Since a pastor's authority in the church is derivative, the question becomes "Do the people trust this leader enough to give him or her the power to operate?" Roy Price, pastor of The Alliance Church, Paradise, California, has done a great deal of thinking about trust:

"My experience has been that real authority comes only out of a trust relationship. I've been in churches where trust between pastor and congregation was nonexistent and also where there was a high level of trust, especially between pastor and board. The difference in what I was able to accomplish was great.

"One church held an underlying suspicion about any new program or idea. That meant a hesitancy to accept my leadership.

"I learned my lesson there. Since then, one of the first things I do in every new charge is get a reading on the level of trust. To do that, I have to get to know the people. I spend informal time with them. The more I know them (and they know me) the more trust will grow—unless there's a total mismatch, in which case I shouldn't be there.

"Another good time for this is prayer times together. We learn a great deal about one another from listening to prayer requests."

It sounds so simple. Where do most pastors go wrong?

"By rushing the process. It takes time. A lot of time. My error when I was younger was wanting to move too fast, making changes I thought needed to be made. But the people weren't ready because they didn't know me."

Price wrote the following chapter in a previous pastorate. He continues to study the process of measuring trust potential in a board or committee and developing trust in the early stages of a ministry. It is a complex but vital task.

had been in the church only a few weeks when the message was as clear as a highway billboard with flashing spotlights: *We don't trust you.* Not everyone felt that way, but I knew I was on trial. The next three years were among the most agonizing I'd spent in twenty-two years of pastoral work. The attendance dropped each year, and with it, a loss of receipts. Two years in a row yielded red-ink reports. There was little visible response to the messages—a traditional barometer. I became aware that one leader wanted to find another pastor.

For the first time in my ministry, I chose not to run from the problem. But the inner agony was tremendous. Doubts of all sorts flooded my mind. Did God call me to this church, or did I act impulsively? Was I called to pastoral work at all? Maybe I ought to throw in the towel and take up another field of work. Everything I tried to do seemed fruitless. Evangelism programs brought literally no results. For every new person gained, it seemed two left.

During this period, I had to ask a staff member to find another place to serve, a task I never imagined I'd face. The church board had agreed to allow me to buy a home when I first discussed a call with them. They later reversed that decision, citing low attendance and finances as reasons. All of this came as a personal ego blow and a challenge to my ability to lead. At the root of the problems was a lack of trust in me. I had failed to evoke trust on the interpersonal level and as a pastoral leader.

The Problem Is More Than Meanness

Why don't people trust their pastors or church leadership? Many times it's simply because they have been burned. Dishonesty heads the list of culprits. It covers a large scope of things from withholding information to manipulative techniques.

For example, one pastor claimed a vision from God to validate a fund-raising idea. His laymen had difficulty refuting the plan. They didn't like the idea, but they submitted with a wait-and-see attitude—how could they fight God? It did not take them long to realize they had been manipulated, and trust was undermined.

That wasn't the kind of thing I was doing. I was not pulling tricks out of a hat or pursuing amorous delights. Nor was I aware of possessing a Napoleonic complex. But I was new. They did not know me, and I did not know them. Thus they didn't trust me.

One day I mentioned my frustration to a member. She said, "Do you really expect people to trust you automatically because you were called here?"

"I thought that came with the job," I said.

"Some of us have been burned, and we need time to get to know you," she responded.

Nearly four years later I learned the story behind her statements. Her husband was a PK. The presbytery where his dad ministered became dominated by a leftist group of seminary professors and pastors. He battled the issues as an involved layman. He watched with anger as his father's stand for conservative theology was gradually discredited.

A few years later this same PK went through a hellish nightmare with a close neighbor. The neighbor had been very active in a local church; he had gone to bat to get the pastor a significant salary increase and actively supported pastoral programs. Then he found the pastor was carrying on an affair with his wife. My friend not only spent hours with his neighbor helping him through this traumatic crisis but had to battle his own feelings of antagonism toward clergymen.

While I was not involved in either situation, his attitude toward me was affected. Others had destroyed trust in the clergy that I had assumed was already mine.

The Ingredients of Trust

I have come to some conclusions about how trust is developed between people. It parallels our relationship with God. Trust is defined as "a firm belief in the honesty, truthfulness, justice, or power of a person or thing." The Greek word for faith is similar. *Pistis* is a "firm persuasion, a conviction based upon hearing."

Why can we trust God? Because he is honest. Because history has proven the reliability of his Word. There are two bases for this confidence. One is the holiness of God's character. The other is his faithfulness. Fulfilled prophecy, the history of Israel, and the life, death, and resurrection of Jesus Christ combine to state emphatically that God is faithful. He can be trusted to do what he says he will do. Knowing this, I hope for a future of blessedness. As A. W. Tozer said, "The tempted, the anxious, the fearful, the discouraged may all find new hope and good cheer in the knowledge that our Heavenly Father is faithful."

Holiness and faithfulness are qualities we too can share. God commands us to be holy. Since holy means "to be whole," it is a synonym for integrity. Moral wholeness means keeping our promises, being honest in all personal and business transactions, and maintaining moral purity.

Why can't our word be as good as God's? Isn't that what

Jesus meant when he said our yes should be yes and our no, no? We need not swear by heaven or earth. To promise to remember someone in prayer just to acquiesce to a request is not honest. We must be faithful to our commitments in ministry, finances, conversation, and with our family.

Recently, my associate paid me the highest compliment I have ever received. "If there's one word I would choose to characterize you," he said, "it would be *integrity.*" I asked him why. He cited these instances: When he candidated for the position of associate, I was quite candid about the problems in the church. I did not conceal my personal struggles or the church's deep needs. He felt I could have snowed him with the positive and sidestepped the negative, but to him that would have diminished my integrity.

In contrast, he told me about a pastor who always talked about the great things in his church until, by contrast, my associate felt like a failure. But when he talked with the man's assistant pastor, an entirely different picture of the church emerged.

My associate also pointed out how I relate to people who are dissatisfied with me. Although I'm friendly, I don't pretend we're best friends. He called it "warmth with reserve." To him it was better than pretending there was no dissatisfaction.

The last thing he mentioned was my transparency to him and the congregation regarding my strengths and weaknesses. Well, I was feeling pretty good by this time.

Then he said that if I were to preach on hospitality in the home, he would inwardly react by saying, *Wait a minute, Roy. You need to be a better model before you exegete that subject.* I have hidden behind various justifications; my wife's work helps pay for college costs, and she doesn't have the time or energy for entertaining many guests. I think our reasons are legitimate; yet his observation is equally valid.

Submission to authority is a part of integrity. When the centurion came to Jesus for his servant's healing, he asked the Lord just to speak the word and it would be done. Referring to his own authority as a commanding officer, he said he could assign a man to a task and it would be done. What was the source of his authority? He was in submission to the one over him. "I myself am a man under authority, with soldiers under me." He knew Jesus had an integrity that came from submission to authority. The result was a power in ministry that the centurion recognized.

I recently asked the board for permission to lead a tour group to Israel. On my own I had booked the tour and had begun recruitment when I became aware of a board member's reservation about it. I reacted. I was reimbursing the church for all postage, stationery, and clerical time, and I was taking vacation time to go. Why should I bring it to the board?

Because it is over me. So I submitted.

Later, I learned that a leading pastor in our city had developed a large tour business a few years ago. Though he had gotten full board approval, the matter was not adequately communicated to the congregation. The press had made it front-page news. My board member was only seeking my protection. The lesson was simple: Be open and trusting with your board, and they will protect you.

Integrity is not a one-shot transaction. Consistency makes integrity active day after day. When I ran into problems in former churches, I conveniently found God calling me to other places of ministry. By sticking it out this time, I have won the confidence of the congregation. Several members have written encouraging notes expressing appreciation for my perseverance. Sensitive and supportive people exist in every church. One anonymous note read, "I appreciate your courage and persistence during a time of great stress." I needed that.

Lewis B. Smedes said, "Personal integrity in a minister is an indispensable quality, yet it comes only with great struggle. . . . Dulling the cutting edge of honesty is really very easy. Masks get comfortable very soon. Roles are learned terribly fast. Ministerial cosmetics go on quickly." A pastor who keeps to the basics will earn respect and trust over the long haul, while the magnetic smooth-talker fumbles his way to another parish.

Trust Takes Time

Southern Baptists have found that a pastoral crisis occurs about every eighteen months of ministry. An interesting corollary is that SBC pastors move on the average of every eighteen to twenty months. In my denomination the average pastor stays only between three and four years. Inconsistency is a large part of this crisis.

Most pastors like to change existing programs and introduce new ones shortly after beginning a new ministry. I've found that you can effectively change things only after your consistency has laid a solid base of trust for you. Without that base, the congregation can become alienated and create a pastoral crisis.

A lay leader took me to lunch one day. While talking about the concerns of the church, he opened my eyes when he commented, "Pastor, let us get to know you before you try to change things." He was pleading for the development of trust so change could be understood and accepted. Instituting adult electives, reorganizing the executive board, and launching a remodeling project had been too much, too soon. Concern about the changes was the outward manifestation of the problem. Could I be believed? Was I a leader who knew what I was doing? Was I willing to slowly demonstrate my integrity?

These questions emphasize a parallel truth. It takes time to build trust because it takes time to know another person. Those of us—and I include myself—who do not have enough close personal contact with our congregations face tremendous obstacles in developing trust. Lack of time, escalating transportation costs, and too many responsibilities are obstacles that must be overcome in developing a trust relationship with people.

The PK I mentioned earlier waited a respectable length of time before he committed himself to me. Time was needed.

He has since become a close friend and confidant. Had I been a short-term pastor, the relationship would never have developed. How unfortunate that just when people and pastor are getting to know each other, he often terminates the romance.

Another contributing factor to trust is transparency. Empathy aids transparency. People need to know that they matter and that their pastor cares about what is going on in their lives. Aloofness will not get a pastor into the heart of the people. It takes more than just understanding them. Jesus is a great high priest because he is touched with the feeling of our weaknesses. We trust him with our problems because we know he cares.

I am strongly committed to the Scripture as having answers for the needs of people. Yet I have learned that helping is more than preaching, and preaching is more helpful after listening. My chance to preach comes regularly; opportunities for the congregation to express their burdens and frustrations come only in personal conversation.

I listen in the foyer and try to ask people about their families, jobs, or personal lives. I listen at committee meetings. I listen in personal conversation. I listen in counseling. By listening, I've nurtured trust. If the trust level is high enough, any suggestion or support will likely be received.

Respect for the rights and integrity of other people strengthens transparency. Am I consistently acknowledging the self-worth of others?

Genuineness is fundamental to transparency. A. W. Tozer wrote of the disease of artificiality: preachers intoning their sermons with an unnatural voice or speaking with vagueness, and avoiding anything that might backfire on them. Tozer demanded: "Every man who stands to proclaim the Word should speak with something of the bold authority of the Word itself. The Bible is the book of supreme love, but it is at the same time altogether frank and downright. Its writers are never rude or unkind, but they are invariably honest and entirely sincere."

Finally, genuineness requires that we lay aside our super-spiritual masks, our pseudosuperior roles as the clergy, and be what we are—people redeemed by the blood of Christ. Many will want us to play a role, and it is often safer to do so than to disclose our struggles. One study has stated that "appropriate self-disclosure has a large number of benefits: increased trust, increased liking (and often, loving), increased attraction, and increased mental health." But those results carry the risk of rejection and loss of control over others.

Am I the Type to Be Trusted?

Recently I became aware of the basic difference of temperament and style between my predecessor and me. He was a warm, fatherly, person-centered pastor. Acceptance, kindness, and understanding were readily communicated. I've always seen myself as friendly and somewhat extroverted. Only recently have I understood that I am task-oriented rather than people-oriented. I work hard on research and sermon preparation and have a gift of teaching. A few meaningful relationships satisfy my social needs.

The difference in our counseling ministries has made this apparent to me. Whenever I've talked with him about the church, he has frequently made reference to the heavy counseling load he had. It's the exact opposite for me, a matter that has generated some criticism. There is less demand for my counseling here than any other place I've ministered. I've wondered why.

One evening I was talking with a psychologist in the congregation about this matter of trust and some of the struggles I've gone through. Though he had heard the former pastor only once, he contrasted the two of us with uncanny accuracy.

Those attracted to the former pastor must have found me distant and aloof at first. Under such conditions, trust is smothered. Had I understood those dynamics earlier, I might have avoided a great deal of trauma and introspection. I may not have behaved differently, but I would have understood the dynamics between the congregation and myself.

Pastors are not the only ones at fault if trust does not develop. Simply stated, pastors too have been burned by their people. Insensitive, callous remarks about preaching style and content or personal matters have driven many people from pastoral work.

After fifteen months in my first pastorate I was just another statistic, fully washed up. I had been criticized for "not preaching with enough love," for poor sermon construction, for not visiting enough, and for not being an effective administrator. One evening as I parked the car I prayed, "Lord, let me get through this board meeting without some hint of criticism."

At the closing prayer I sighed with relief. While I was preparing to leave, two leaders of the church stopped me and in effect said, "Pastor, don't you feel your wife could be more outgoing?" They were sincerely trying to help a twenty-four-year-old and his wife, but criticism wasn't the way to accomplish their purpose. I slammed the file cabinet shut, angry enough to fight.

"I hope you don't feel we've been too hard on you," one said.

"Too hard?" I replied. "I certainly do. You men have criticized about every area of my work. In criticizing my wife you've gone too far."

I resigned. I had no place to go. I was broken in spirit, confused, and crushed in heart. Eventually, God brought healing and led me back into pastoral work.

That experience, joined with other events, caused me to become more withdrawn and distant. I have been wary of church boards, fearful of rejection, and hesitant to disclose myself ever since. Obviously, my attitude has not been an aid to building trust. But there is something to be said for a man's accepting what he is and working with that. If God shaped the events of my life, perhaps he could do through me what he could not do if I were a different type. If that is so, then I must accept the fact that an intimate counseling-centered ministry is not for me.

I still need trust, though. Integrity and faithfulness aren't built upon temperament. And trust is a two-way street. Integrity and faithfulness are fundamental to pastor and people alike. Absent in either party, trust languishes. Present—or at least developing—in both, trust flourishes. The benefits are cooperation, peace, and a freedom of relationship that is contagious.

Who is responsible to see that trust is developed? The pastor is—if you're the pastor. The layman is—if you're the layman.

SEVEN

SELF-DISCLOSURE: HOW FAR TO GO?

For the early Christians
koinonia *was not the frilly*
fellowship of church-sponsored
biweekly outings.
It was not tea, biscuits,
and sophisticated small
talk in the Fellowship Hall
after the sermon. It was
an unconditional sharing of
their lives with the other
members of Christ's body.

RON SIDER

"There's no better way of building trust with a new congregation than through self-disclosure."

The speaker is Em Griffin, professor of communication at Wheaton College in Illinois. For him, self-disclosure opens the door to all kinds of relational progress. But there are ground rules. He explains further:

"My idea of an agreeable person is a person who agrees with me. Identification is the name of the game. And if I don't know you, I can't identify with you.

"Now there's always the danger that if I let you know me, you'll be turned off. For instance, if I share doubts on scriptural authority and you're high on scriptural authority, that will make trust unlikely. But if I don't reveal my attitudes, background, and fears, you won't have any handles to get to know me. Trust is filling in the blanks."

Em remembers an experience with a pastor friend that reinforced the lesson of self-disclosure.

"I always had a certain amount of respect for him, because I knew he served a difficult urban parish. But I didn't know him well until we were together at an Inter-Varsity conference. We ended up spending about six hours together in the conference, eating breakfast, riding a bus, even ducking out of a couple of sessions just to talk.

"As we grew closer, he told me about a close friend who had just moved away; he missed the friendship badly. He also told me about a time he was mugged outside his church one evening. Guys were lying in wait for him. When he didn't have any money, they pistol-whipped him. He shared the fear and bitterness he felt for months afterward.

"Those disclosures immediately drew me to him, and we have formed a very close friendship. We get together once a month for a half-day retreat. Neither of us has the time for it, of course, but we do it to survive by sharing one another's lives. All this was stimulated by those first disclosures.

"Sharing doesn't have to be confessional, although it often leads to that. It's a sharing of story; not history, but intimate thoughts, feelings, and emotions."

Has sharing always been easy for Em Griffin?

"It's easy now, because I've gotten so many positive strokes through it, and a lot of good things have come to me as a result. I had a prof at Fuller Seminary, Edward Carnell, who first modeled it for me. Toward the end of his life he was really hurting, but instead of hiding it, he talked to his students about it. Although he was a very shy man, you could tell he was making an effort at fellowship. And that's what it led to. It didn't come across at all as whining or complaining. It seemed entirely appropriate, and he drew us into his life through it."

Em Griffin has never forgotten that early experience. He maintains to this day that self-disclosure is an essential step in getting to know people anywhere.

In my first year of high school, I double-dated with my older sister and her boyfriend. We were at a coffee shop when Ralph commented that I looked flushed. As a matter of fact I did feel hot, and headachy as well. Ralph pointed out that during the evening my face had broken out even more than my teenage acne warranted. When I admitted that the lights in the restaurant seemed a bit bright, he announced the obvious. I had measles.

This was a blow. Our family was scheduled to leave on a Florida vacation the next morning. My sister and I knew that as soon as our parents discovered my illness, they would cancel the trip. So we conspired not to let them know. I took aspirin for the headache, covered my arms with long-sleeved shirts, and wore dark glasses outside. I stayed out of the sun and used generous quantities of talcum powder and Clearasil to mask the worst blemishes on my face. My folks never found out.

Although this was an extreme example, it represented my basic philosophy toward self-disclosure as I grew up. Summed up, it would be, "Don't tell Mom!" Early patterns die hard. Today, whenever I experience strong emotions, my initial impulse is to guard my words and label my feelings TOP SECRET.

I now feel another pull, however. I am a college professor, youth leader in my church, Young Life national board member, and father. In each of these roles I know the loneliness of leadership, and I find myself uncomfortable adopting a detached stance. I have a strong desire to take others into my confidence and openly report what is going on inside me.

I'm torn, and I find that I'm not alone. The world can be a scary place. We're hesitant to share our innermost thoughts with others. Some people are willing to commit their hopes and frustrations to the pages of a diary, but the diary has a lock and is stored in a private place. Others share their dreams and disappointments with a dog or favored pet. Unless we make the mistake of spilling our guts to a mynah bird, our secrets are safe with them.

But neither of these routes is completely satisfying. Even prayer doesn't fulfill our desperate need to be known and loved by other warm human beings. Still we hold back. Why? John Powell answers that question simply in his book *Why Am I Afraid To Tell You Who I Am?* "Because if I tell you who I am, you may not like who I am, and it's all that I have."

I picture a giant Mardi Gras masquerade ball. The couple has been together all evening, and the man is entranced with this mysterious partner. As midnight approaches he pleads, "Take off the mask—that's all I ask." She finally complies, and he's stunned! "Put back the mask," he shouts. That's what we fear.

Being a Christian does not automatically make it easier to reveal our true selves. Because we have some God-given standards of what life should be, it may be even harder to let others glimpse the person inside. I heard a respected Christian leader once say there's more fellowship in the average bar than in the Christian church. He suggested we take the advice of James seriously: "You should get into the habit of admitting your sins to each other" (James 5:16, Phillips).

I was intrigued by the idea of a systematic program of self-disclosure, and I shared my excitement with a fellow student. "Aw, that's nothing new," he said. "My roommate and I have a pact. I tell him his sins, and he tells me mine." This kind of judgment makes most Christians leery of self-disclosure. We're afraid of getting dumped on. And we have a sneaking suspicion God's opinion is reflected in man's judgment. The pastor or Christian leader has an additional worry. He lives in a fishbowl. Won't it invalidate his ministry if his followers know what he's really like? It seems safest to merely pray and keep one's own counsel.

Psychologist Sidney Jourard believes most people have a tough time sharing the deep parts of their lives with even one other person. The body pays the price of silence. Headaches, back pains, ulcers, colitis, high blood pressure are forms of protest. They are tilt signals—indications that something is out of kilter. Jourard sees these and other illnesses stemming from the lack of self-disclosure:

> In thinking about health, I like to conjure up the image of a family of germs looking for a home in which they might multiply and flourish. If I were the leader of such a family of germs and had the well-being of my family at heart, I would avoid any human like the plague so long as he was productively and enjoyably engaged in living and loving. I would wait until he lost hope, or became discouraged, or became ground down by the requirements of respectable role-playing. At that precise moment, I would invade; his body would then become as fertile a life-space for my breed of germs as a well-manured flower-bed is for the geranium or the weed (*The Transparent Self*).

Jourard advocates taking the risk of sharing our attitudes, reactions, loves, fears, and background with at least one significant other. He believes a more tranparent lifestyle will promote intra- and interpersonal well-being. Do I agree? That's what the rest of this article is about.

Benefits of Self-Disclosure

One of my favorite movies of the last decade was *The Sting*. Robert Redford and Paul Newman play two Depression-era con men who bilk a big-time New York mobster out of a million dollars. They go to fantastic lengths to carry out their deception. The tension keeps you on the edge of your seat throughout the movie, knowing that one little slip in an unguarded moment will bring the whole ruse crashing down on them.

What strikes me most is the fantastic psychic energy required to live a lie. Honest self-disclosure relieves this tension. I can relax if I don't need to constantly monitor what parts of my life I have metered out to which people.

Pastors and counselors have known for years that tension release accompanies self-disclosure. Clients come to them for "the talking cure." They seek a sympathetic ear, not advice. By honestly revealing their inner life, they leave feeling more whole. This is unique in the health profession. I know of no claim that taking a patient's blood pressure will cure him of hypertension. Yet taking the pulse of the soul not only indicates mental health, but the very act often brings relief. This same release is as available when talking to a friend over coffee as in a professional's office at fifty dollars an hour.

There's a second benefit for the person who takes the self-disclosure plunge. He or she becomes known. A high school girl brought this home to me. After leading a Young Life club for a decade, I announced one night that I was in my final year. Laura was in tears after the meeting. She said, "Oh, Em, I'm so sad. Now we won't get to know each other." I tried to placate her by pointing out that we went to the same church and I was friends with her folks. I assured her she'd have ample opportunity in the future to get to know me. "That's not it," she responded. "I want you to get to know me."

Christians have a special need to be known. It's natural for someone with moral sensitivity to conclude he's invented sin. When guilt feelings hit, I have a hard time believing God forgives unless I first experience forgiveness from some warm bodies here on earth. But even that acceptance is hollow unless I've been transparent enough to know that people see the real me—warts and all. Otherwise I'll figure they love me only because they don't really know how rotten I am. Being open and honest with others gives me the assurance that no matter how people react to me, they're responding to the genuine article, not some spruced-up version.

Self-disclosure offers a third plus. In the process of letting someone else get to know me, I discover who I am. You'd think it would work the other way around—that I'd first figure out who I am, then let others in on the secret. But the two are often simultaneous. Paul Tournier, the noted Swiss physician, states we can't get to know ourselves through introspection. Introspection is like peeling the skin off an onion; you remove layer after layer and discover there's nothing left.

Instead, Tournier claims that dialogue with others is the only true route to self-knowledge. He practices what he preaches. Recently this famous Christian doctor and writer invited a group of college students to have tea. The students were overwhelmed at the time and effort he invested in preparing and serving the food. Couldn't these hours have been spent more profitably writing or doing something more important? Not according to Tournier. He simply said, "There is nothing more important than honest dialogue between Christians. It's how we discover ourselves, our friends, and our God."

Finally, self-disclosure usually draws us closer to those who listen. True, there's no guarantee it will work that way every time; people can get turned off when they hear too much, too fast, from too many. But a certain amount of openness is a necessary condition for interpersonal intimacy.

It's not clear why personal sharing fosters attractions. It may be that people discover just how similar they are. Or perhaps it's a response to the gift of trust inherent in self-revelation. I feel privileged when you let me in on something close to you. It makes for a special bond. That's especially important for leaders. They tend to be separated from their people by a status gap. Appropriate self-disclosure is a way to bridge that gulf.

I've listed a number of reasons for lowering our guard and revealing ourselves to others. These are compelling ideas to me. But there's obviously another side to the story. Prudence requires that we examine the possible pitfalls involved in openness.

Dangers of Self-Disclosure

Self-disclosure can boomerang. Folks may get a glimpse of what I'm really like and decide they want no part of me. Jimmy Carter dropped ten points in the polls when he confessed lustful tendencies in a *Playboy* interview. Research findings confirm that overdisclosure can dampen attraction. We avoid the bore who wants to discuss every detail of his latest operation. Perhaps that's our gnawing fear—that others will find our self-disclosure merely tedious.

Negative reactions hurt. Yet more distressing is the possibility that what we've told in private may be leaked in public. When I was in seventh grade, I told a new friend about one of my hobbies—building miniature ballparks. I would lay out the foul lines with chalk, erect the outfield fences with building blocks, and fashion the double-deck grandstands with materials from a steel girder construction set. I copied the dimensions of Wrigley Field and built a replica of Comiskey Park, complete with working light towers. The day after I told Don, it was all over school: Em was doing something weird with Tinker Toys. That hurt.

The professional recipients of secrets in our society are the clergy, doctors, and lawyers. They are sworn to uphold an ethic of confidentiality. Rarely is this obligation violated. But when we entrust our confidences to the lay person, there's a greater chance of exposure. To some, the value of a secret comes when it is spilled to others.

Another danger of self-disclosure is that people can be hurt by our candor. The term *brutal honesty* has come to describe the bludgeoning technique of telling others things for their own good. When the offended party objects, the insensitive talker responds self-righteously, "I was only being honest."

I don't want to offend others this way. I knew one woman who would say whatever entered her mind. If I walked into the room and she didn't like my tie, she'd say so for all to hear. People tended to overlook her bluntness as a form of eccentric behavior. But if hurting people is central to self-disclosure, I want no part of it.

Others balk at the idea of voluntarily giving away what they consider their greatest personal resource—privacy. South American Indians object to being photographed, believing the camera robs them of a portion of their essence. Greta Garbo voiced the desire of many when she said, "I want to be alone." Seclusion became an obsession for Howard Hughes. Although not many go to such extremes, a significant number of people regard solitude as healthy. They figure there's a good chance they'll regret tomorrow the careless words bestowed today.

An attack on the whole concept of self-disclosure comes from Christians who are suspicious of the philosophical roots of humanistic psychology. They look at some of the leading proponents of openness and honesty in human relations—Carl Rogers, Erich Fromm, Rollo May, Abraham Maslow—and see these men advocating such things as:

• Unconditional acceptance, which seems to be ethically bankrupt.

• Self-love, which they label narcissistic and/or idolatrous.

• The basic goodness of man, which plays fast and loose with the concept of sin.

And thus these people reject self-disclosure as a practice tainted by the humanism of the Me Generation. Other Christians don't want to toss out the idea of transparency, but they're disturbed by the cult of confessionalism that is very willing to report sin but makes little effort to repent of it.

I hope by now you're convinced that self-disclosure is

neither an unmitigated blessing nor an automatic curse. That's too simplistic. The question of whether to reveal personal history, private thoughts, and hidden emotions is not one of either/or. Rather it's one of appropriateness.

Appropriateness can be viewed from three angles. One has to do with the recipient of your openness—the *who*. It makes sense to differentiate between those who will lend a sympathetic ear and those who can't handle intimate discussion. The timing of self-disclosure is a second consideration—the *when*. The right time and place makes both parties feel more comfortable. Finally, there's the matter of how much honesty—the *what*. Some things may be best unsaid. Others need airing. How can the who, when, and what aspects of appropriate self-disclosure work together to maximize the benefits of openness while minimizing the drawbacks?

Who Will Be the Few?

We're easily fed up with the game playing, masks, and phoniness in the world. It's tempting to react by throwing our hands up in despair and committing ourselves to spill our guts to everyone. But we can't. It's impossible to establish a meaningful relationship with a toll collector—the result would be a monumental traffic jam.

Most of our relationships are destined to be governed by roles—the social lubricant that makes normal interaction possible. We can and should play things straight with all people, but intimate self-disclosure needs to be reserved for the few. We have only so much time and psychic energy.

Whom should we choose? *Someone we trust.* It would be folly for a player in a high-stakes poker game to show his hand, since the other players are out to do him in. By contrast, there are people, often part of the Christian community, who have our best interests at heart. They feel forgiven, are comfortable with themselves, and aren't eager to persuade us to change. Slow to judge, they unconditionally accept us for who we are, even if they don't agree with all our actions. Any time you run across a person radiating this kind of warmth, it's worth taking the self-disclosure plunge.

Confidentiality is part of trust. You'd think that getting burned on the disclosing end would make us doubly careful not to violate the trust implicit in a shared secret, but reality compels us to recognize we often get sloppy in holding a confidence. Discretion is a cultivated response—it's not innate.

Returning to the poker analogy, prudence dictates that we not bet more than we can afford to lose. This means placing a tentative trust in a person and checking how he handles it. If he violates that trust, we will be sadder but wiser. If he respects our privacy, we can then entrust him with more. It's reminiscent of Christ's statement: "He who is faithful in a very little is faithful also in much" (Luke 16:10, RSV).

There's a well-known fact of sharing called the "bus rider phenomenon." People often prefer to bare their soul to a stranger rather than to a lifelong friend. The reason is obvious: There's no risk involved. Although this kind of self-disclosure affords some catharsis, it doesn't give us any of the interpersonal benefits. And, it's risky. How do we know that person isn't a friend of a friend? Often this temporary relief is overshadowed by doubts and embarrassment the morning after. It's much more satisfying to select a listener with whom we have an ongoing relationship.

I'm fortunate that my pastor is my best friend. We've been close for ten years. Every week we spend an hour and a half in the steam room at the local YMCA. Our continuing friendship means the intimate details of my life that swirl together with the vapor are heard in the context of mutual responsibility. My pastor's lucky, too. Although I'm active in the youth program of our church, I'm not an elder or deacon, simply an unofficial "steam room committee member." He can use me as a confessor, cheerleader, or sounding board. Because we have a history of many soggy hours together, neither of us feels on stage with each other.

My wife and I experienced this same accountability at a

marriage retreat. Six couples shared struggles of faith, vocation, sex, money, conflict, and parenting between themselves and among each other. Self-disclosure wasn't cheap. Material shared during the weekend was still known by significant others a week later. It placed emphasis on authenticity.

Appropriateness dictates that we have a sliding scale of disclosure. Jesus revealed much about himself to the multitudes, but a great deal was unsaid or masked in parables. The disciples heard more. But only the inner circle of Peter, James, and John viewed Jesus on the Mount of Transfiguration. We also need to be sensitive to those who hear our disclosure, and to the times when they can't handle our truth. "I have yet many things to say to you, but you cannot bear them now" (John 16:12). This is not the despairing cry of a rejected leader but the discerning observation of one who's attuned to others.

When to Take a Chance

A poster on my office wall pictures a long-necked turtle. The caption reads: "Behold the turtle, who makes progress only when he sticks his neck out." Many advocates of self-disclosure use a turtle as an example of what *not* to be—retreating into his shell because he's afraid to expose himself to others.

But I see this funny-looking creature as a model of appropriate disclosure. Picture two turtles—face to face—with their heads almost completely hidden. One turtle extends his neck just a bit. If the other turtle responds in kind, the first one ventures out some more. In a series of minute movements the first turtle ends up with his head in the sunshine, but only if his counterpart follows his lead. At any time he's prepared to slow the progression, come to a complete stop, or even back off.

There are a number of salient features in my turtle picture. First and foremost is reciprocity. At best, self-disclosure is not a solo act. There is a *quid pro quo*: You tell me your dream, I'll tell you mine.

Research confirms that the healthiest form of self-presentation is just slightly ahead of the norm. I've tried to capture this idea in the image of my first turtle. He takes the initial risk. He's always a tad ahead of the game—testing, probing, hoping. But at the same time he's constantly monitoring the other's response and is ready to pull back when confronted with indifference or hostility.

Reciprocation is a crucial indication of the other's internal state of mind. It signals that he's not offended by my initial revelation, and even more important, it shows a willingness to be vulnerable. There's a parity of risk: I've got the goods on him just as much as he does on me. Reciprocation also reveals a readiness to proceed to deeper levels of intimacy.

The turtle model also focuses on the gradual nature of appropriate self-disclosure. It takes time. Stress conditions can accelerate the friendship process, but the normal pattern is one of slow growth.

The tortoise imagery doesn't address the question of public self-disclosure. Is there ever justification for a leader to spread his or her life out like an open book in the pulpit, classroom, or office? If my own experience is any indication, the answer is yes. In 1976 I published a book called *The Mind Changers: The Art of Christian Persuasion*. I included many personal examples to illustrate my points. I've received a number of letters from people who've read the book. The theme of the correspondence is invariably the same: "Thanks for being willing to reveal who you are."

Groups often place their leaders on pedestals. Self-disclosure helps them come down from that position and become warm human beings who laugh, sweat, fear, and go to the bathroom just like everybody else. It's a trade-off. What they lose in status, they gain in approachableness. When a leader's authority is in question, self-revelation is counterproductive. But when competence is recognized, vulnerability is a strength.

I've taught an intensive, two-week wilderness seminar in group dynamics. After dinner each night, one of the eight participants takes from thirty mintues to an hour to present the significant past events that have shaped him or her up to now. We call it "This Is Me." There's no question that this exercise does more to leapfrog the group into an intimate knowledge of one another than any other activity we do.

The success of this sharing is partially due to the fact that I go first. Since disclosure begets disclosure, I try to model a comfortable depth of sharing that encourages others to do the same. Another factor in its effectiveness is the distinction between *history* and *story*. History is a recitation of facts. If I tell you, for instance, that my older brother died of pneumonia before I was born, that's history. It's quite possible you would voice a mental *So what?* But if I tell you my parents were deathly afraid I'd catch cold and therefore overprotected me by dressing me in a snowsuit when it was 45 degrees, that's the beginning of story. It's even more helpful when I tie this in with my present casual disregard for preventive health measures. I've interpreted the facts and told how they've affected me. Story is a big part of what self-disclosure is all about.

Emotions and Self-Disclosure

Feelings are the great leveler of human existence. You may be from a farm, have earned the Ph.D. in theology, vote Republican, and enjoy golf. I may be a product of the inner city, drive a fork lift at a box factory, agitate for social reform, and be a bowling nut. We disagree in starting point, method, and conclusion. Yet we both taste the fear of rejection, the surge of sexual attraction, the weariness of responsibility, and the warmth that comes with affirmation. Since we all are equal on the gut level, feelings are the common currency of self-disclosure.

Emotions are also like the ocean surf—powerful, exciting, and often scary. Thus, we naturally tend to self-inject a mental Novocain that will numb our passion, dampen our fear. That's too bad. I agree with John Powell's approach: "Emotions are not moral, neither good nor bad in themselves. If I am to tell you who I really am I must tell you about my feelings whether I will act upon them or not. With rare exceptions emotions must be reported at the time they are being experienced" (*Why Am I Afraid to Tell You Who I Am?*).

This is easy to say but hard to do. I was in a sharing group with students in my school when I felt a stab of bitter jealousy toward another professor. I was caught in a dilemma. Intellectually I'm committed to Powell's advice, but green-eyed envy isn't a socially acceptable reaction in my fellowship. My discomfort was compounded by the fact that the teacher's wife was a member of the group.

I don't know what tipped the balance, but somewhat haltingly I reported my feeling. The reaction was immediate. She laughed, but not in derision. That very morning her husband had confessed to her how he coveted my ease with students. My jealousy vanished immediately. Wouldn't it have been sad if I'd held it in and nurtured a grudge? It would have been even more tragic—and sinful—if I'd given in to resentment and cut him down in front of students. Prompt reporting of the emotion was the better part of wisdom. My goal is to act as wisely in the future.

The jealousy I just spoke of was *my* problem, not his. But what if someone does things that are irksome? Perhaps he talks with his mouth full or boasts so much about his accomplishments that others are turned off. Does honest self-disclosure involve sharing our irritation?

The answer, I think, depends on the nature of our relationship. My standard is this: I stick to compliments unless the other person has in some way contracted for negative feedback. I have no right to pop somebody's balloon unless he's indicated a willingness to hear my criticism. Of course, there may come a time when actions go beyond the point of being merely bothersome. If through ignorance or malice someone starts to hurt people, simple human justice requires that you speak out.

A person can signal in a variety of ways that he's up for negative feedback. Close friendship is one. The other day I told my steam room friend that his breath smelled of garlic. He thanked me, and he meant it. The trust we've built with one another took the sting out of my words.

A direct request can also give permission. I read the first draft of this article to my class and asked for comments, stressing my desire for criticism so I could improve it. After an awkward pause one fellow said, "Well, as long as you asked . . ." and initiated a string of helpful suggestions.

In all of the above cases, it's important to state our opinion as just that, not as truth thundered down from Mount Olympus. "You're a prude!" is not nearly as helpful or loving as "I get the impression you're embarrassed when we speak of sex." A certain tentativeness is appropriate. We may be way off base. Sharing our perceptions is more loving than announcing our judgments. God's first call is not to worship honesty but to love.

Keeping quiet is not usually our problem. Most of us err on the side of nondisclosure. We constrict our circle of confidants, fail to recognize situations where openness is appropriate, and censor thoughts that would be quite acceptable. It's natural to be cautious.

But we of all people have reason to open more of our lives to public view. Our transparency can reveal the love of Jesus, which reaches out in concern to others. Our self-disclosure may bring about a reciprocal relation with someone who needs to know Christ's love personally. Through all of this, with Jesus as our model, we may find our lives considerably enriched.

EIGHT

A BUDGET PRIMER

*Two-thirds of all the strifes,
quarrels, and lawsuits in
the world arise from one
simple cause—money.*

J. C. RYLE

The misuse of money blocks more ministry in the local church than any other single cause. The reason may be too much money, too little money, or misuse of just the right amount of money, but the result is the same: fractured relationships and spiritual atrophy. A pastor taking a new church had better get the financial picture of the church well in hand before anything else is attempted.

That's not to say the pastor must solve all the church's money problems. But he must be aware of them and have a clear understanding with the key leaders on how they are to be handled. If this base isn't covered, relational and spiritual programs will be sabotaged.

As district superintendent of the Church of the Nazarene's Michigan District, Neil Strait has counseled many pastors on church money problems. He knows the many flavors of pickles a pastor can get into.

"A fundamental axiom for a pastor changing churches: Look over the last two or three financial reports to see the relationship of receipts to bills. That sounds pretty simple, but it's amazing how often it's overlooked. Getting a handle on the unpaid bills is a big problem for many churches. It's not that a pastor should make his decision whether or not to take a church (if that's his decision to make) based on this information. It's just that he needs to know the status of the church's financial condition, or he can't function effectively.

"Not all problems of this sort are caused by pastoral neglect. You'd be surprised how often the church treasurer is reluctant to give the pastor, especially if he or she is young, all the financial information. Sometimes the reason for this is the dismal state of the books; sometimes it's because the treasurer sees this as a personal power base; sometimes it's an honest attempt to keep the pastor from 'soiling' his hands with 'worldly' concerns. But even pastors who delegate all financial functions need to know the status.

"This isn't a problem that faces young pastors only. Recently the treasurer of one of our churches refused to give a treasurer's report to the church board. The pastor, new to that church but a veteran of several years, didn't know what to do. So he asked me to attend a board meeting.

"I met with them and at one point asked outright, 'What's the balance in the treasury?'

"The treasurer said, 'We've got some money.'

"I repeated the question, and he gave the same answer. I had to ask him five times before he would give it to me. Finally, after we had dragged it out of him, I asked him why he was so reluctant to tell.

"He said, 'I've been church treasurer here for forty years, and here you are, a stranger, coming in and prying.' After looking deeper into the situation, we finally decided there wasn't anything malicious about it. He just considered it his domain. It was an extreme case of a treasurer who didn't feel the pastor could handle financial matters."

Twice a year Strait conducts a seminar on church finances for young pastors. The enthusiastic response has convinced him that the fundamentals of good budget control are among a pastor's most important tools for ministry, whether in a new pastorate or at any point.

Lhe young pastor sat with his wife, staring blankly through the tears. The dream that had led him to his first pastorate had become a disaster. His problems stemmed from church finances, and he took little comfort in the fact that many young pastors before him had failed for similar reasons.

John had little financial expertise. His family was well-to-do, so finances had seldom been discussed in the home. His college and seminary training were underwritten; thus some important learning experiences were by-passed. The few courses about church management in seminary had been elementary, and he hadn't thought much about church finances. Now the day of reckoning had dawned, and all the challenge and romance of ministry seemed to fade.

Financial problems cast a heavy spell over all they touch. It's essential for a pastor to develop good financial tools to properly handle church finances. Here are some basic steps in handling the finances of your church in these economy-chaotic days.

Work Out a Budget

A budget establishes the priorities for ministry and improves money management. It also provides a periodic review toward goals achievement. The church budget reveals what the congregation thinks is worth an investment.

Three considerations should be made:

1. Carefully select the people who fashion the budget. If developed by a group whose sole purpose is to save money, a lot of ministry and not a little future will be sacrificed. Input should come from church leaders who are on the front lines of making ministries happen and also have the future growth and spiritual development of the church at heart.

It's been said, "Nontithers cannot have the same vision for a church as tithers." The giving base of a growing church in my district consisted mostly of those who were deeply dedicated to evangelistic outreach. Most of them gave beyond the 10 percent tithe. However, the board had invited some newer members into the financial planning session, hoping to involve them in a meaningful way.

As the session got down to the nitty-gritty of working out the budget, several of the newer members voiced opposition to budget expansions. Some of the core group talked to them about "giving a little more" for outreach, but the idea was received with resistance. The level of commitment, to a large degree, does determine final dollars in a church budget.

2. Budgets also should be put together by those who may not know finances but know the church's priority for ministry. Although others may be experts in percentages and cash flow, they will miss the point of ministry if they are overly concerned with mechanics.

One church asked three of its members who worked in the financial world to prepare its budget for the coming year. When it was returned to the board, it had severe cuts and adjustments. Although financially sound, it presented a number of ministry problems. When the board discussed the various allocations, three things surfaced:

• The finance committee had given more attention to investing escrowed funds than funding for ministry.

• They had built in recession anticipations, ignoring inspiration giving.

• They had eliminated programs on a dollar-for-dollar basis instead of their usefulness in ministry.

3. The finalized budget must be the gauge for all spending. It's of little value to organize, plan, and underwrite a budget if it's going to be disregarded. Although a planned process to approve extra expenditures is important, a church must learn to live within its budget.

An ambitious pastor I knew laid his dream for an expensive ministry before his church board. Some of the members saw the potential but asked for time to consider it; some pointed out the present budget would not be adequate for the ministry. They advised the pastor to scale down the plan to fit within the budget and then complete the dream sometime in the future.

The young pastor ignored the signals. He rallied a group around his plan and forged ahead. Needless to say, the budget couldn't begin to handle it. Monies needed for utilities and current operating expenses were now threatened by other irons in the fire, and when the board met to discuss the problem, strong voices were raised. A sharp division split the board, and three families left the church.

In retrospect, the pastor saw his mistake. Had he lived within the budget for the year and built his dream into a long-range plan, he could have had his plan *and* his people.

Consider Zero-Based Budgeting

Zero-based budgeting simply means totally re-evaluating each section and ministry when preparing the coming year's budget instead of simply adding a certain percentage to the existing categories. This helps promote those ministries that have produced results and eliminate those whose usefulness is over.

A downtown, traditional church in the East with a declining membership called a young pastor to its pulpit. He hadn't been there long when he called for a brainstorming session with the leaders. The pastor shared two reasons for the meeting: one, to find out where the church was in its mission and to chart its future; two, to identify its purpose and establish priorities before the budget was designed for the coming year.

In-depth discussions followed over the next few months. In preparation for the budget, the pastor requested that zero-based budgeting be used. He then set up several committees to research the existing ministries of the church. To the surprise of several, some of the oldest programs were programs in name only—they had ceased to be relevant. Another group was at work identifying potential ministries. They studied the community, assessed its needs, and explored how their church could minister to those needs.

When the budget committee met, it was able to delete dead-end ministries and incorporate meaningful ones. Zero-based budgeting had forced the church to see itself for what and where it was, and then chart a course of mission and growth.

Insist on Accountability

Gone are the days (or they should be gone) when the treasurer used to count, deposit, pay out, and raise money without anyone asking a question. No one on the finance team of the local church should be exempt from accountability. Three things result when accountability is built into the church organization:

1. Risks are kept to a minimum. Every church likes to feel it is corruption-proof, but churches are not exempt from temptation, dishonesty, and evil schemes. Controls should be established to eliminate potential problems by separating various jobs. For example, the person who writes checks should not be assigned the responsibility of authorizing the expenditures.

2. Groups and individuals are kept from building a power base. Church treasurers often feel as though they own their

church's money, and many are extra stingy with facts about the church's financial status. Trust is earned when the treasurer is required to make regular detailed financial reports; accountability confirms ability and character.

A church in a small Ohio community discovered its treasurer of forty-three years had been mismanaging funds. Over several months an officer of the youth group had been placing funds with the treasurer to be escrowed for a trip they were planning. When the funds were requested to purchase tickets and complete other travel arrangements, the girl was told the fund was $1,800 less than she had figured.

Her father went over her books to make sure she hadn't made a mistake. When he requested a meeting with the treasurer to help them find their error, the treasurer refused to make the books available, even when requested to do so by the pastor and members of the board. Within the week the stately, white-haired treasurer resigned in disgrace. A stunned church thought it couldn't happen. Periodic accountability would have caught the problem much earlier.

3. Regular audits benefit and protect not only the church but the treasurer too. Insist on yearly audits, and have them done by a qualified accountant. Although in-house audits will save you money, they won't tell all you need or want to know about the financial records.

Honesty is important in both the budget and the financial records. Keep in mind these three points:

• Don't hide an item in the budget. Make sure "Miscellaneous" doesn't get so big it raises bigger questions than you can adequately handle.

• Don't solicit funds for one cause and use them for another.

• Don't change the figures to make them look good.

Monitor the Finances

If you're the pastor of a church without paid help, your job of monitoring is gigantic. If you pastor a larger congregation with paid bookkeepers and financial expertise, your job of monitoring can be delegated but is still important. Monitoring the budget keeps the church and its financial goals on course.

To monitor doesn't mean to be a watchdog over all expenditures; it means all facets of the budget are reviewed regularly and corrections are made when needed.

At least four items should be covered through monitoring the church budget:

1. Cash flow. This makes funds available for immediate use without having to borrow, and it makes them available for emergencies, improvements, or pending bills.

Whether we know it or not, cash flow tells us several things about what's happening in the church:

• It's an indication of stewardship; the acceptance of mission, ministry, and purpose by the congregation.

• When it decreases, it's the first warning sign that something might be wrong either with the economy or the church. Proper follow-through will give adequate time to check out matters as well as correct any malfunction in the church by scaling back expenditures and/or developing ways to increase income.

• When it increases, it might be the signal that ministries can be improved or expanded without awaiting the year-end accounting report.

2. Accounts payable. They simply must be kept up to date. This doesn't mean all bills are paid; it does mean that nonbudgeted items are not paid in place of budgeted items. If many budgeted items are held in abeyance in favor of payment of nonbudgeted items, deficit spending will occur.

One church had a substantial insurance payment coming up. During the same period, several church members were advocating a night of special music, which would cost about the same amount as the insurance bill. They felt if they would hold the bill, pay in advance for the music groups, and then take an offering the night of the concert, they could have the special music as well as the money for insurance. Well, there was a blizzard the night of the concert, and only a handful of people showed up. Less than $100 was raised; the insurance bill could not be paid.

3. Budget percentages. One should know as much about the percentages as the total dollars. Dollars raised and/or spent are meaningless unless they are placed against the number of months left in the budget. Before expenses can be scaled back or new components added to the existing budget, the decrease or increase must be put into the perspective of the entire year.

4. Legitimacy of expense. This is an area where close monitoring pays off in dollars and cents. It was not uncommon when I was a pastor to have my secretary/bookkeeper catch a bill mailed to our church that should have gone to another "First Church" in a neighboring town. By monitoring our expenses and researching undocumented bills, we saved hundreds of dollars.

Communicate the Financial Picture

Too often, the only time we talk to the congregation about finances is when money is needed. They need to know the total picture, which includes the blessings. Communication creates a feeling of ownership in parishioners. The money comes from those who sit in the pews, and they have a right to know about the financial situation.

One Midwest pastor had a slide presentation designed that graphically portrayed the intent and purpose of each budget item. Through such visuals the members identified the items and were able to see how they fit into the total purposes of the church.

A woman in my former church was remarkably gifted in drawing cartoons. She offered her talents to present the need for library funds to the congregation through overhead transparencies that depicted people reading, listening to tapes, and using other resources from a library. Her drawings showed our people the benefits of improving the library, and as a result, more funds were allocated for this ministry.

However one chooses to communicate the financial picture of the church, one thing is certain—the congregation will get a message. If there is little communication, the message will be shrouded with suspicion, uncertainty, and questions. The congregation's response to opportunities is determined to a great degree by the financial message given.

Watch Investments

Not all churches need to worry about investing, but some need to consider it as a wise transaction. A church with inactive or escrowed funds should consider investing them in treasury bonds or whatever vehicles afford the most interest for shortest amounts of time and greatest security.

The following checklist is helpful regarding investments:

1. Determine what monies can or should be invested.

2. Determine if investment should be short-term or long-term.

3. Research investment potential. Use the services of a financial consultant who has some knowledge of the mission and methods of the church.

4. Determine before investing how income from such investments will be used.

5. Build in safeguards such as immediate access to investments in case of an emergency.

6. Keep investment research up to date especially on long-term investments to realize greatest potential of yield. Guard against the investment that is 100 percent secure, yet inflation-prone due to its low yield.

7. Keep the church board informed of all investments.

8. Don't let the enticements of investments pull money away from meaningful ministries, thus thwarting the outreach of the church.

Allow Room for Growth and the Unexpected

In all the financial planning and control, save room for dreams, growth, and the unexpected as well as for faith. Not all intrusions into the budget are hostile. Sometimes a church is presented with an opportunity of faith, and it needs to have an available vehicle to respond to these opportunities without wrecking the budget. The "love offering" concept is one way. Where the hearts and purses of God's people are open in love, the church will meet the needs God makes known.

A pastor I know in the West has been at his church three years. He followed a free-spending pastor who had brought the church almost to financial collapse. My friend did three things—none of them profound—that turned the church around financially. He asked the church to set a budget and live within it; he communicated the financial needs and opportunities of the church, speaking of future goals instead of past failures; and he set up proper guidelines for monitoring and accountability.

The church is now growing and giving more than it ever has. Because this pastor has put the financial house in order, he can give greater amounts of time to outreach and ministry, both of which will add to the financial base of the church.

NINE

A DANGEROUS SIDE EFFECT TO MOVING

The Christian leader's chief occupational hazards are depression and discouragement.

JOHN R. W. STOTT

When it comes to spotting hidden snares in the ministry, Carl F. George demonstrates a practiced eye. Now director of the Charles E. Fuller Institute of Evangelism and Church Growth after more than a decade of pastoring, he spends major blocks of time with individual churches and pastors who request his help.

He especially watches for things most people miss. For example, public success on Sunday morning doesn't tell the whole story of a ministry, he says. "Almost all ministers are well educated theologically. Most seminary graduates have more to teach than anybody wants to learn. If we spend any time at all preparing for a given sermon, we will meet the needs of the listeners. As Dan Baumann, author of a widely used preaching textbook, says, 'Anyone who simply sets forth the text and gives its meaning distinctly will be accused of freshness.'

"Meanwhile, the serious deficiencies are in management and leadership skills. This is a decision that goes unmade."

In the following chapter, Carl George puts his finger on a life management skill that is badly needed following a transition.

Pastors who change churches sometimes get more than they bargained for.

They naturally have become comfortable with a set of familiar faces in a church. Although the demands of preaching, leading a staff or committees, visiting parishioners, and counseling are at times overwhelming, the old church is still basically an affirmative setting. The pastor is needed and valued. He or she has many opportunities to offer help, encouragement, appreciation, and to receive expressions of appreciation ("strokes") in return. The people have come to a place of trust.

When the pastor shifts to another church, the relational network has to be rebuilt with strangers. This reduces, for a time at least, expressions of appreciation. The period of fewer strokes often triggers a mood alteration now termed clinical depression.

This is not necessarily harmful or threatening. Depression is a normal human response to stressful life changes, a reaction to the loss of something valued and familiar or to an uncertainty about the future. (Even success—the accomplishment of a long-sought goal—can sometimes lead to feelings of depression.) A job transition that removes a person from familiar people who are loved is exceedingly stressful, though new challenges may mask this stress for a time.

Clinical depression can occur in two forms.

1. Acute depression is felt immediately after a change in life situation; it often hurts deeply, but its cause can be readily identified (another example: the sudden death of a spouse).

2. Sometimes the depressive reaction is delayed, perhaps because the person is preoccupied. When the actual depression (known as the chronic form) sets in, it occurs at such a distance from the causative event (as much as two years later) that the person does not connect the two. He wonders why he should feel so bad for no apparent reason.

The transitional minister often finds himself plagued by this question. The following symptoms, though occurring without obvious cause, should be considered indicators of depression stemming from the job transition. (Note: No one is likely to experience all these symptoms, and some of them can be experienced in different ways by different people.)

- Sleeplessness (or sometimes oversleeping)
- Loss of appetite and weight (or sometimes compulsive overeating)
- Loss of sexual desire (or sometimes the temptation to take a fling)
- Lowered self-esteem; feelings of uselessness
- Hurting all over inside, wanting to cry (and perhaps being unable to)
- Apathy; losing interest in the things you used to care about
- Difficulty in making basic decisions you normally make quickly
- Unexplainable shifts in mood, unconnected to daily events
- Withdrawal from people, even though you desperately want company
- Physical tension: headaches, pains, muscle cramps

- Inability to begin important projects
- A sense that time drags on, passing very slowly
- Unresponsiveness to events and people
- Decline of spiritual life (or sometimes increased fervor)
- Occurrence of suicidal thoughts
- Hypersensitivity to rejection
- Inability to concentrate
- Loss of spontaneity
- Fatigue
- Increased sickness

Underlying these behaviors is the fact that the depressed person has lost perspective on life and doesn't know how to regain it. Not recognizing the depression, he does not see that it is only temporary and will eventually subside. The new pastor in particular may tend to misread his troubles and unhappiness, explaining them instead in one of the following terms:

Being out of God's will. Either he was presumptuous to accept the position (for which he now thinks he is unsuited), or denominational officials made a mistake in recommending him for it.

Personal spiritual shortcomings. Since Christians "aren't supposed to have these kinds of feelings," either he has backslidden or is lacking faith.

Satanic oppression. (There may in fact be some of this, but it is probably not the entire explanation.)

Family unhappiness. His family may be experiencing changes and stress, too, and the pastor may see his blues as a response to the family's struggles.

Slipping health. These symptoms "must be" the first foreboding signs of a serious, debilitating illness.

Ten Ways to Cope

Once depression is recognized as depression, what can be done to overcome it? Mostly we endure it as a necessary process of grief, knowing it will eventually end. But certain steps can be taken to help cope with the experience in the meantime.

1. *Remind yourself that in time, this too shall pass.* Christian mystical writers in centuries past have referred to these crises as "the dark night of the soul." Nights do not last forever.

2. *Realize that depression, like any change, offers an opportunity to grow.* You will be a fuller, more mature person, with godly personal qualities refined and basic values intensified, for having gone through the experience.

3. *Realize you are not alone.* Others experience similar struggles, too.

4. *Remind yourself that God has not abandoned you and that you are where he wants you to be.*

5. *Rebuild your "stroke level" at home:* touching and holding your spouse (with or without sexual relations), touching and being touched by your children.

6. *In your work, reinforce the sense of team participation whenever possible.* Share your schedule with your staff; have office prayer meetings; assign team work projects.

7. *Seek inward healing through God's Word and from his Spirit;* sing (aloud or silently) favorite hymns or worship choruses.

8. *Re-read the biblical accounts of leaders, paying particular attention to their emotional upheavals.* Your experience is not so different from that of Elijah, Moses, David, or Paul.

9. *Seek ways to offer verbal affirmation and appreciation to others, especially at the collegial level.* The Golden Rule applies to compliments, notes of appreciation, and words of encouragement, too.

10. *Seek help.* Although transitory in nature, depression may be an acutely serious problem. Medical and psychiatric professionals are finding many new ways to treat depression. Utilize their gifts.

Selected Bibliography

Albrecht, Karl. *Stress and the Manager: Making It Work for You* (Englewood Cliffs, N.J.: Prentice-Hall, 1979). An application of stress theory to the manager's role and work environments.

Feinberg, Mortimer R., Gloria Feinberg, and John J. Tarrant. *Leavetaking: When and How to Say Goodbye* (New York: Simon & Schuster, 1978). Popular-level anecdotal work with suggestions for responding to life crises.

Flach, Frederic F. *The Secret Strength of Depression* (New York: Bantam, 1975). A thorough and balanced treatment of the subject, written for the lay reader by an eminent psychiatrist.

Hart, Archibald G. *Coping with Depression in the Ministry* (Arcadia, Calif.: Cope Publications, 1980). Discussion kit with tapes. Available from Charles E. Fuller Institute, Box 989, Pasadena, CA 91102.

Hart, Archibald G. *Depression: Coping and Caring* (Arcadia, Calif.: Cope Publications, 1981). Book and kit with tapes. Available from Charles E. Fuller Institute.

TEN

THE UNBUSY PASTOR

*Our vocation is to live
in the Spirit—not to be
more and more remarkable
animals, but to be the
sons and companions of God
in eternity.*

ANTHONY BLOOM

Although the pressures of going to a new church may force a pastor into a certain singlemindedness for six to twelve months, balance must still be maintained. The essential pastoral task must not be sacrificed to administrative concerns. Family life cannot be sacrificed. The well-rounded edges of our personal lives must not be squared to sharp, irritating points.

If you talk to Eugene Peterson, for the past twenty-one years pastor of Christ Our King Presbyterian Church in Bel Air, Maryland, you quickly discover he is a man who reads mysteries, extracts theological insights from classic novels, runs marathons, and goes for long hikes in the woods with his wife. But he has not always been so diverse in his interests.

"One of the worst years I ever had was in the early days of this church. Our building was finished, and I realized I wasn't being a pastor. I was so locked into running the church programs I didn't have time. One of my kids said, 'You haven't spent an evening at home for thirty-two days.' She had kept track!

"I was obsessive and compulsive about my administrative duties, and I didn't see any way to get out of the pressures. So I went to the Session one night to resign. 'I'm not doing what I came here to do,' I said. 'I'm unhappy, and I'm never at home.'

"Well, the Session didn't want me to resign, and I really didn't either if I could get back to pastoring. Together, we worked out a solution. I would trust them to run the church, and I would concentrate on being a spiritual leader. That's what I've done ever since."

In a book that tells you how to do something—the whys and wherefores of changing churches—it's important not to let you think for a minute that this process should change who you are. Eugene Peterson talks about this in the following chapter.

The one piece of mail certain to go unread into my wastebasket is the one addressed to the busy pastor. Not that the phrase doesn't describe me at times, but I refuse to give attention to someone who encourages what is worst in me.

I'm not arguing the accuracy of the adjective; I am, though, contesting the way in which it is used to flatter and express sympathy. "The poor man," we say. "He's so devoted to his flock; the work is endless, and he sacrifices himself so unstintingly." But the word *busy* is the symptom not of commitment but of betrayal. It is not devotion but defection.

The adjective *busy* set as a modifier to *pastor* should sound to our ears like *adulterous* to characterize a wife, or *embezzling* to describe a banker. It is an outrageous scandal, a blasphemous affront. Hilary of Tours diagnosed our pastoral busyness as *irreligiosa solicitudo pro Deo*, a blasphemous anxiety to do God's work for him.

I (and most pastors, I believe) become busy for two reasons; both reasons are ignoble.

I Am Busy Because I Am Vain

I want to appear important. Significant. What better way than to be busy? The incredible hours, the crowded schedule, and the heavy demands on my time are proof to myself—and all who will notice—that I am important. If I go into a doctor's office and find no one waiting, and see through a half-open door the doctor reading a book, I wonder if he's any good. A good doctor will have people lined up waiting to see him; a good doctor will not have time to read a book, even if it's a very good book. Although I grumble about waiting my turn in a busy doctor's office, I am also impressed with his importance.

Such experiences affect me. I live in a society in which crowded schedules and harassed conditions are evidence of importance. I want to be important, so I develop a crowded schedule and harassed conditions. When others notice, they acknowledge my significance, and my vanity is fed. The busier I am, the more important I get.

I Am Busy Because I Am Lazy

I indolently let other people decide what I will do instead of resolutely deciding myself. I let people who do not understand the work of the pastor write the agenda for my day's work because I am too slipshod to write it myself.

But these people don't know what a pastor is supposed to do. The pastor is a shadow figure in their minds, a marginal person vaguely connected with matters of God and good will. Anything remotely religious or somehow well-intentioned can be properly assigned to the pastor.

Because these assignments to pastoral service are made sincerely, I lazily go along with them. It takes effort to refuse, and there's always the danger the refusal will be interpreted as a rebuff, a betrayal of religion, and a callous disregard for people in need.

It was a favorite theme of C. S. Lewis that only lazy people work hard. By lazily abdicating the essential work of deciding and directing, establishing values and setting goals, other people do it for us; then we find ourselves frantically, at the last minute, trying to satisfy a half dozen different demands on our time, none of which is essential to our vocation, to stave off the disaster of disappointing someone.

But if I vainly crowd my day with conspicuous activity, or let others fill my day with imperious demands, I don't have time to do my proper work, the work to which I have been called, the work of pastor. How can I lead people into the quiet place beside the still waters if I am perpetual motion? How can I convincingly persuade a person to live by faith and not by works if I have to constantly juggle my schedule to make everything fit into place?

*   *   *

If I'm not busy making my mark in the world and not busy doing what everyone expects me to do, what do I do? What *is* my proper work? What does it mean to be a pastor? If I had no personal needs to be fulfilled, what would I do? If no one asked me to do anything, what would I do? Three things.

I Want to Be a Pastor Who Prays

I want to cultivate and deepen my relationship with God. I want all life to be intimate—sometimes consciously, sometimes unconsciously—with the God who made, directs, and loves me. And I want to be a person in this community to whom others can come without hesitation, without wondering if it is appropriate, to get direction in prayer and praying.

I want to do the original work of being in deepening conversation with the God who reveals himself to me and addresses me by name. I don't want to dispense mimeographed handouts that describe God's business; I want to report and witness out of my own experience. I don't want to live as a parasite on the firsthand spiritual life of others, but to be personally involved with all my senses, tasting and seeing that the Lord is good.

I know it takes time to develop a life of prayer: set-aside, disciplined, deliberate time. It isn't accomplished on the run, nor by offering prayers from a pulpit or at a hospital bedside. I know I can't be busy and pray at the same time. I can be active and pray; I can work and pray; but I cannot be busy and pray. I cannot be inwardly rushed, distracted, or dispersed. In order to pray I have to be paying more attention to God than to what people are saying to me; more attention to God than to my clamoring ego. Usually, for that to happen there must be a deliberate withdrawal from the noise of the day, a disciplined detachment from the insatiable self.

I Want to Be a Pastor Who Preaches

I want to speak the Word of God that is Scripture in the language and rhythms of the people I live with. I want to know the Scriptures thoroughly, personally, intimately, and then be able to say them again to the people around me. I am given an honored and protected time each week to do that. The pulpit is a great gift, and I want to use it well.

I have no interest in "delivering sermons," challenging people to face the needs of the day, or in giving bright, inspirational messages. With the help provided by scholars and editors, I can prepare a fairly respectable sermon of that sort in a couple of hours or so each week, a sermon that will pass muster with most congregations. They might not think it the greatest sermon, but they would accept it.

What I want to do can't be done that way. I need a drenching in Scripture; I require an immersion in biblical studies. I need reflective hours over the pages of Scripture as well as personal struggles with the meaning of Scripture. That takes time, far more time than it takes to prepare a sermon.

I want the people who come to worship each Sunday to hear the Word of God preached in such a way that they hear its distinctive note of authority and know their lives are being addressed on their home territory. A sound outline and snappy illustrations don't make that happen.

This kind of preaching is a creative act that requires quietness and solitude, concentration and intensity. "All speech that moves men," contends R. E. C. Brown, "was minted when some man's mind was poised and still." I can't do that when I'm busy; there's too much happening. When I am busy I can prepare and deliver clever, well-outlined, readily understood sermons; when I am busy I can be a fairly creditable cheerleader, rallying people to the cause of righteousness, quite often to the satisfaction and even the praise of my congregation. But I can't preach when I am a busy pastor.

I Want to Be a Pastor Who Listens

A lot of people approach me through the week to tell me what is going on in their lives. I want to have the energy and time to really listen to them so when they are through, they know at least one other person has some inkling of what they're feeling and thinking.

Listening is in short supply in the world today; people aren't used to being listened to. I know how easy it is to avoid the tough, intense work of listening by being busy, letting the hospital patient know there are ten more persons I have to see. Have to? But I'm not indispensable to any of them, and I am here with this one. Too much pastoral visitation is punching the clock, assuring people we're on the job, being busy, earning our pay.

Pastoral listening requires unhurried leisure, even if it's only for five minutes. Leisure is a quality of spirit, not a quantity of time. Only in that ambiance of leisure do persons know they are listened to with absolute seriousness, treated with dignity and importance. Speaking to people does not have the same personal intensity as listening to people. The question I put to myself is not "How many people have you spoken to about Christ this week?" but "How many people have you listened to in Christ this week?" The number of persons listened to must necessarily be less than the number spoken to. Listening to a story always takes more time than delivering a message, so I must discard my compulsion to count, to compile the statistics that will justify my existence.

I can't listen if I am busy. When my schedule is tight and crowded, I'm not free to listen: I have to keep my next appointment; I have to get to the next meeting. But if I provide margins to my day, there is ample time to listen.

*   *   *

"Yes, but how?" The appointment calendar is the tool with which to get unbusy. The appointment calendar is a gift of the Holy Spirit (unlisted by Saint Paul, but a gift nonetheless) that provides the pastor with the means to get time and acquire leisure for praying, preaching, and listening instead of just doing. It is more effective than a protective secretary; it is less expensive than a retreat house. It is the one thing everyone in our society accepts without cavil as authoritative. The authority once given to Scripture is now ascribed to the appointment calendar. The dogma of verbal inerrancy has not been discarded, only reassigned.

When I appeal to my appointment calendar, I am beyond criticism. If someone approaches me to pronounce the invocation at an event, and I say, "I don't think I should do that; I was planning to use that time to pray," the response will be, "Well, I'm sure you can find another time of the day to do that." But if I say, "My appointment calendar will not permit it," no further questions are asked.

If someone asks me to attend a committee meeting, and I say, "I was thinking of taking my wife out to dinner that night; I haven't listened to her very carefully for several days," the response will be, "But you are very much needed at this meeting; couldn't you arrange another evening with your wife?" But if I say, "The appointment calendar will not permit it," there is no further discussion.

The trick, of course, is to get to the calendar before anyone else does. Mark out the times for prayer, for reading, for leisure, for quietness, for emptiness, for silence and solitude, out of which, and only out of which, creative work—creative prayer, creative preaching, creative listening—can issue.

I find that when these central needs are met, there is plenty of time for everything else. And there is much else. For the pastor is not, and should not be, exempt from the hundred menial tasks, the trivial errands, the necessary duties, or the administrative humdrum. These also are pastoral ministry. But the only way I have found to accomplish them without resentment and without anxiety is to first take care of the priorities. If there is no time to nurture these essentials, I become a busy pastor, harassed and anxious, a shining, compulsive Martha instead of a contemplative Mary.

A number of years ago I was a very busy pastor and had some back trouble that required therapy. I went for one-hour sessions three times a week. No one minded that I wasn't available those three hours. Everything still got done. Because the three hours had the authority of an appointment calendar behind them, they were sacrosanct.

On the analogy of that experience, I venture to prescribe appointments for myself to take care of the needs not only of my body but also my mind and emotions, my spirit and imagination. One week, in addition to daily half-hour conferences with Saint Paul, my calendar reserved a two-hour block of time with Fyodor Dostoevski. My spirit needed that as much as my body ten years ago needed the physical therapist. If nobody is going to prescribe it for me, I will prescribe it for myself.

*   *   *

In Herman Melville's *Moby Dick*, there is a violent, turbulent scene in which a whaleboat scuds across a frothing ocean in pursuit of the great white whale. The sailors are laboring fiercely, every muscle taut, all attention and energy concentrated on the task. The cosmic conflict between good and evil is joined: chaotic sea and demonic sea monster versus the morally outraged man, Captain Ahab.

In this boat is one man who does nothing. He doesn't hold an oar; he doesn't perspire; he doesn't shout. He is languid in the crash and the cursing. This man is the harpooner, quiet and poised, waiting. And then this sentence: "To insure the greatest efficiency in the dart, the harpooners of this world must start to their feet out of idleness, and not out of toil."

Melville's sentence is a text to set alongside the psalmist's "Be still, and know that I am God" (Ps. 46:10), and alongside Isaiah's "In returning and rest you shall be saved; in quietness and in trust shall be your strength" (Isa. 30:15).

Pastors know there is something radically wrong with the world. We are also engaged in doing something about it. The stimulus of conscience, the memory of ancient outrage, the challenge of biblical command involve us in the anarchic sea that is the world. The white whale, symbol of evil, and the crippled captain, personification of violated righteousness, are joined in battle. History is a novel of spiritual conflict.

In such a world, noise is inevitable, and immense energy is expended. But if there is no harpooner in the boat, there will be no proper finish to the chase. Or if the harpooner is exhausted, having abandoned his assignment and become an oarsman, he will not be ready and accurate when it is time to throw his javelin.

Somehow it always seems more compelling to assume the work of the oarsman, laboring mightily in a moral cause, throwing our energy into a fray we know has immortal consequences. And it always seems more dramatic to take on the outrage of a Captain Ahab, obsessed with a vision of vengeance and retaliation, brooding over the ancient injury done by the Enemy. There is, though, other important work to do. Someone must throw the dart. Some must be harpooners.

The metaphors Jesus used for the life of ministry are frequently images of the single, the small, and the quiet, which have effects far in excess of their appearance: salt, leaven, seed. Our culture publicizes the opposite emphasis: the big, the multitudinous, the noisy. It is, then, a strategic necessity that pastors deliberately ally themselves with the quiet, poised harpooners, and not leap, frenzied, to the oars. There is far more need that we develop the skills of the harpooner than the muscles of the oarsman. It is far more biblical to learn quietness and attentiveness before God than to be overtaken by what John Oman named the twin perils of ministry, "flurry and worry," for flurry dissipates energy and worry constipates it.

Years ago I noticed, as all pastors must notice, that when a pastor left a neighboring congregation, the congregational life carried on very well, thank you. A guest preacher was assigned to conduct Sunday worship, and nearby pastors took care of funerals, weddings, and crisis counseling. A congregation would go for months, sometimes as long as a year or two, without a regular pastor. And I thought, *All these things I am so busy doing—they aren't being done in that pastorless congregation, and nobody seems to mind.* I asked myself, *What if I, without leaving, quit doing them right now? Would anybody mind?* I did, and they don't.

ELEVEN

BURNING OUT, RUSTING OUT, OR HOLDING OUT?

*Do not despise your situation.
In it you must act, suffer, and
conquer. From every point on earth,
we are equally near to heaven
and the infinite.*

HENRI AMIEL

Changing churches provides a unique opportunity to re-evaluate your work style in light of God's goal for your ministry. One is never more open to changes in style than at the change points of life.

The unique feature of the ministry workload is its open-ended nature. There is far more to do than time to do it in. So the pastor is faced with questions such as: What's enough? What's lazy? What's "working too hard"? The answers can determine not just how you adjust to a new church but your prospects for the long haul. James Berkley, pastor of Dixon (California) Community Church at the time he wrote the following chapter, remembers his experiences with those questions.

"There was a time in my first year when I thought I wasn't going to make it. The senior pastor called me into his office and said, 'The youth group really isn't going like we expect it to.' Suddenly, I had visions of washing out of the ministry right there. It came as a shock. I didn't realize things weren't going well.

"I had to reassess what I was doing. I asked myself if I was working as hard as I could. I got input from other people who knew me well. They thought I could do more. So I knuckled down and worked harder. It made me be much more thoughtful about what I was doing.

"I wasn't lazy. It's just that I didn't know what was expected. The *truth is, I was there three years, and the youth groups were all right, but they never took off like you read about in books. There was always that edge of worry lurking somewhere.*

"But as I continued to work in ministry, I realized another side to the productivity question. A minister could work too hard and burn out. This came home to me as I watched other pastors eat themselves alive in ministry. I said to myself, 'I don't want to be like that.' They were reverse role models.

"I remember one guy here in Dixon who made me look sick in the amount of work he turned out. But he left town quickly under some kind of cloud. He accomplished a great deal in a short period of time but hurt the church far worse in the process."

In this final chapter, Berkley addresses the question of how much work is enough.

A few months ago a friend of mine—one of the most gifted and effective ministers I have ever met—very nearly drove his car off a bridge. Intentionally. The pressures of ministry ate to the core of this young pastor of a thriving church. He mentally composed a farewell message, determined the best freeway bridge for his purposes, and planned the final escape that would neatly conclude his depressed existence.

But before he got in his car, he remembered he had an appointment. Instead of suicide, he dutifully attended a committee meeting.

Another friend serves a small church with large problems. When I asked how the ministry was going, a long sigh best described his feelings. He is not sure how long he can take it.

Still another pastor, young and dedicated, admits to a succession of stomach ailments. Every contact he makes, every decision, every responsibility finds its way to his viscera. Antacid manufacturers love him.

So many pastors enter their calling with superior training, gifts, talent to spare, and all the drive in the world, only to be pressed through the ministerial sieve. Great dreams turn into defeat, despair, exhaustion, and ulcers. As I number the casualties, I often wonder, "Is disaster inevitable?"

British evangelist Christmas Evans once declared, "It is better to burn out than to rust out!" I admire the bravado. It sounds dedicated, bold, and stirring. However, when I view the burnt-outs and the almost burnt-outs who lie by the ecclesiastical road, the glory fails to reach me. I see pain and waste and unfinished service. Is there not a third alternative to either burning out or rusting out? In Acts 20:24, Paul stated, "I consider my life worth nothing to me, if only I may finish the race and complete the task the Lord Jesus has given me." Herein lies the model I choose to follow. I want neither to burn out nor rust out. I want to finish out the race.

I want to survive this decimator called the ministry. I want something to remain of this person after ten or twenty or thirty more years. It is not that I lack dedication; I just desire something worthwhile to use as the years go by. I fail to see the splendor of a church-ravaged shell weeping in his office twenty years from now. So let me confess my plan for survival. Perhaps my observations can aid your survival as well, to the end that we may all be counted among the survivors.

Tapped, Not Trapped

An assurance of divine calling and giftedness for ministry ranks first in my ministerial survival formula. If God has not placed me in this slot with the tools I need to do my work, then I do not want to be here! The advice to ministerial candidates remains sound: "If you can possibly be happy in any other profession, do it!" Among the first ministerial casualties are those not called to the ministry. If I am not tapped for ministry, then I will certainly feel trapped in a ministry that overspends my means.

Paul urged Timothy to "fan into flame the gift of God, which is in you through the laying on of my hands." Timothy, reticent as he was, could at least point to a specific time and place where he was called forth and gifted for ministry. How important that call must have been in this shy young man's survival as a pastor.

We all have seen men and women trapped in ministry. They do not belong. They function poorly. They are ineffective, out of step, miserable. I often marvel at their perseverance and shudder at the price they and their churches pay. Somehow the gatekeepers passed them through, but since they were never called by God, everybody loses.

Then I think of a friend who entered the pastorate after an executive career with McDonald's. Even after he finished seminary and served a church for a few years, the hamburger folks wanted him back badly enough to offer him double or triple his salary as a pastor. He agonized over this, contemplating his aged Rambler and five children needing college educations, but he turned the offer down. This man knew he was tapped for ministry. Nothing could lure him away from his calling. Like Paul, he was "compelled to preach. Woe to me if I do not preach the gospel."

I plan to finish out the race because I am convinced God placed me in it. That sense of call is vital to pastoral survival.

A Warehouseman, Not a Warehouse

Several years ago I walked on the Ventura Pier with a pastoral colleague as he wrestled with an overwhelming situation. From all indications, Toby's wife was dying. I asked him how he could possibly cope with the imminent loss of his wife. He had an infant son plus all the regular cares of a pastor, and now this. It seemed too much to me.

With amazing calm, Toby explained, "I consider myself a warehouseman, not a warehouse. I only handle each burden long enough to unload it in the Warehouse. God is the Warehouse; I am the warehouseman." I have never forgotten those simple words.

How often caring pastors accumulate the weight of the burdens they handle. A parishioner is fired. A marriage breaks up. An alcoholic cries for help. A college student is killed in an accident. Piece by piece the burden mounts. Pastors who hold on to everything will soon find their knees buckling. They will eventually be crushed by the load. The more pastors care, the more they open themselves to others, the more effective they are, the more they are weighted down.

How many times have we preached on Matthew 11:28—"Come unto me, all you who are weary and burdened, and I will give you rest"—and yet have felt we must shoulder all the burdens ourselves? We are not warehouses; we are merely the handlers.

Recently a young mother came to me terribly distraught over the stillborn child of a close friend. I acutely shared her distress, but realistically I could tell her nothing she did not already know. I could not neatly wrap up the situation with a tidy solution, and she knew it before she entered my office. Together, we gave it up to God. We placed our concern in the Warehouse. She wanted that, anyway. I carried that burden only long enough to give it to God. I sometimes learn my lessons.

If I heed Toby's advice, I will not be crushed before I finish the race. I may get weary from shuffling the loads. There may be more deliveries than I care to handle, but I will not be crushed if I carry one load at a time just long enough to give it away.

Jethro's Law

Passing the baton to others is the third element of my survival formula. Consider the story of Moses' father-in-law, Jethro, in Exodus 18. This wise man observes Moses doing his day's work.

"Moses," he says (pardon my paraphrasing), "what are you doing? Why are you making all these nice people waste a whole day waiting for you to mediate their disputes?"

"Because they are there," Moses replies perceptively.

Then Jethro hands Moses some sound fatherly advice: "What you are doing is not good. You and these people are only wearing yourselves out. You can't do all this alone. Select capable men, appoint them as judges, and let them handle the simpler cases."

There are few things I do that someone else cannot do as well. For four years I edited our monthly church newsletter. Every article passed under my pen, and too many originated with that pen. No more! I found a woman in our congregation with newspaper experience. She now edits the newsletter, and I have gained nearly a day a month. Why did it take me four years? I think I actually enjoyed playing Moses—busy, important, overburdened—but I finally got tired.

According to Paul in 2 Timothy 2:2, we are to pass along our skills and understandings to others, who will do the same. Jethro's Law is not only an effective way to work, it is the right way. Jesus operated that way, eventually leaving his work to a bunch of amateurs—who changed the course of the world.

Jethro concludes, "If you do this and God so commands, you will be able to stand the strain, and all these people will go home satisfied." Any idea that eases my strain *and* satisfies the people is one I want to heed. I intend not to run alone when I can find co-runners. We can help each other finish the race.

Consecrated Negligence

Perhaps you have tried this idea with your church leaders. Ask them to list the duties they expect you to perform. Then have them allot the number of hours a week you should spend on each task. Combine their lists, total the hours, and you will probably find the sum greater than the hours in a week. If you never eat, sleep, relax, or spend time with your family, you will still have insufficient time for everything somebody expects of you.

I have gradually learned that many tasks will necessarily remain undone. To survive amid this reality, I have cultivated the fine skill of consecrated negligence. Perhaps this is my finest survival technique. Those who fail to learn consecrated negligence squirm in continual guilt or languish in chronic exhaustion. My friend who was ready to end it all over the bridge had tried frantically to be the ideal pastor. As he told me later, he felt driven to do everything possible, to do it well, and to do everything with the same energy and creativity. From my viewpoint, he nearly succeeded, but the personal toll proved unbearable. In his inability to be comfortably negligent in any aspect of ministry, my friend nearly destroyed himself.

Paul found it necessary to defend himself to the Corinthians. He wrote, "Christ did not send me to baptize, but to preach to gospel." Here was a man who understood consecrated negligence. He knew his mission—preaching—and he would not let the Corinthians set his agenda for him. While he preached, Paul remained unapologetic in not baptizing, for it did not belong in his commission.

Mere negligence will never do, however. We must determine our mission through prayer, wise counsel, and experience. But once we have set our priorities with wisdom and spiritual insight, we must stick with them and pursue them with all our energies. If that means missing a committee meeting to call in the hospital, or teaching with less preparation to preach with more, then so be it. I have chosen where I will be negligent, and I can live with it. Consecrated negligence tells me not to run in every race if I intend to finish the race I consider most important.

A Sanctified Sense of Humor

A sense of humor greases the ministerial skids to allow gliding where others grind. One summer I finished a bicycle trip with our youth just in time to attend the Sunday service. Tired, dirty, and out of touch with my calendar after a week on wheels, I fell into bed at home after the service.

A phone call awoke me. "Reverend Berkley, aren't you supposed to be at a wedding now?"

My worst dream suddenly materialized. I had forgotten a wedding! I arrived at the park fifteen minutes late to find a small gathering enjoying the summer day and apparently unconcerned about the time. Whew! How glad I am that I can chuckle over that *faux pas* rather than agonize over my failings.

Certainly the sense of humor should be sanctified. I wince at the rancor and bitterness sometimes passed off as humor. Biting jests only inflame wounds. Insensitive humor often makes matters worse. To enter the hospital room of a critical kidney patient with a snappy "How's the plumbing today?" invites instant rejection. Well-placed humor, however, enlivens dragging board meetings. Glimpsing the humorous angle of a difficult situation provides mental relief. The person who is lighthearted about himself will be transparent and nondefensive in dealing with others. Humor pays its way.

While I run my race, I intend to take time for laughter, especially when I catch a glimpse of myself with egg on my face. That laughter will keep me running.

Three Tractors

My life was given me to spend for God. I have no intention of hoarding it or wasting it, but I do intend to spend this one life wisely. Those who quickly spend the principal in a showy display of sacrifice will have no interest in later years. Genuine martyrs are one thing, but misguided wastrels cut short their ministry in the kingdom.

In my agricultural town, a tractor pull is a big event. The idea is to see which tractor can pull a weighted sledge the greatest distance. The unlimited class boasts behemoths with about as much resemblance to a farm tractor as a dragster has to my Honda. These tractors catch the eye, make a lot of noise, and pull a mountainous weight, but their moment of glory is brief. Sometimes in the midst of a pull the massive engine will dramatically flame out from the strain placed on it. In a moment it is good only for the scrap heap.

In the play yard at our church rests an ancient little tractor embedded in the ground for the children to play on. Long ago it saw its last working day. The spark plugs are fused to the block and the pistons frozen in their cylinders. One day it quit working, and now it is so rusted it cannot work.

On my uncle's fruit ranch in Washington resides another old tractor. This beat-up Ford gave me rides around the orchard nearly thirty years ago, and it still putters around the orchards, hauling bins of apples and mowing hillsides of weeds.

Thirty years from now, I want to be that Ford tractor. I may not make the noise or even accomplish the magnificent feats of the unlimited-class tractor, but I want my motor running for the long haul. Spare me from the ecclesiastical junk pile. However, may my consecrated negligence never turn to pure negligence and make me akin to the playground tractor. I have fields to work for many years. Let me be that reliable and effective little Ford that hauls apples year after year. I don't want to burn out or rust out; I want to hold out, to finish the race.